AF544974

How to Train a Husband

A Vet Tech's Guide
to Love and Marriage

By

Mallary McKinzie LVT

Cover illustration by Cindi Rose

How to Train a Husband is published under Mission books, sectionalized division under Di Angelo Publications INC.

MISSION BOOKS
an imprint of Di Angelo Publications How to Train a Husband; A Vet Techs guide to Love and Marriage.
Copyright 2016 Mallary McKinzie in digital and print distribution in the United States of America.

No part of this book may be reproduced or transmitted in any form or by any means electronic or mechanical, including photocopying, recording or by any other informational storage system, without permission in writing from the publisher.

For information:
Di Angelo Publications,
4265 San Felipe #1100 Houston, Texas, 77027.
www.diangelopublications.com

Library of congress cataloging-in-publications data

ISBN-10: 1-942549-26-1
ISBN-13: 978-1-942549-26-0

Layout: Chris Perez
Printed as POD in the United States of America.
Edition: 10 9 8 7 6 5 4 3 2 1 1.
Fiction---Relationships---Self- Help.
V2. Love and Romance---United States ----
Techniques and Advice.
United States----How to Train a Husband. I. Title

Dedicated to Argyle the terrier,
my first Husband, and to Gabe
the human, my current husband.
To my Pack, simply,
Thank you.

HOW TO TRAIN A HUSBAND

Introduction

You arrive. You walk through the doors to find that they are all lined up and very excited to see you. You survey the room and casually note particulars about each individual. There are short ones and tall ones. Some of them have smooth hair, and some have fluffy or curly hair. Their personalities range from cuddly and shy to tough and aggressive. There are some, you can tell, who will only want to please you. Some will be content to nestle on the couch on a Saturday night, comforting you when you've had a long week. You recognize the ones you will feel safe with and are confident they will protect the house. There are athletic ones that will accompany you on a run and can't wait to head to the park; and right next to the sporty ones are the lazy ones who barely raise their heads when you walk by. Some you see the potential in, but they will obviously need a *lot* of training. Finally, there are a few that clearly need to be neutered. There are many different pedigrees and breeding, a plethora of choices to delight any girl. As you walk by each one, you must decide "Is this the right one for me?" You must trust yourself enough to know you made the right decision, leaving behind the runts of the litter.

Are you at a pet shop or an adoption fair at Pets-R-Us? Nope. It's happy hour at any sports bar in the known universe; and you have a more important choice to make than whether you want a beer or the two-dollar margarita special.

Ladies, a bar is just like a dog shelter, and picking a man is exactly like picking a pup: a choice. Behind each choice you make is a commitment that requires thought, preparation and research. It demands a basic understanding of yourself and your lifestyle, and the confidence to trust yourself in making that choice.

No one wants a puppy forever. Eventually, no matter how adorable they are, you will become exhausted with constant training, correcting, and having your house destroyed and your life disrupted. After the excitement of your cute new companion wears off, your goal will be to focus on the light at the end of the tunnel and put in the work every relationship expects. Soon, this whelp will grow up. He will mature. Every day you can see the effort he is putting forth and the progress he is making on his way to becoming your dream man. If you have made your intentions and expectations very clear, your companion will have learned what you envisioned the relationship would become and will be able to reciprocate with love, affection and obedience.

But, if you don't know what you want, how is your new companion supposed to know? If you are unclear or inconsistent, you can confuse your new partner. Are you sending unclear signals or commands? If you only want your friend to love you, it can further the confusion you both feel. The last thing you want is to spend months or years hiding how you really feel and wind up in a relationship that is more of a charade. Are you so scared of being alone that you would rather live a lie?

Before trying to find a man, you need to fully understand who you are in a relationship and what role you prefer to play. You can't buy a harness without measuring up the pup. You can't successfully potty-train without isolating the problem, even if that problem is you. And if it's not ok for the dog to shit on the carpet, why is it ok for a guy to shit on your heart?

Training a man is much like training a dog. It does not, however, mean that you will be able to change who he is. "Opposites attract" is not a foolproof mantra. A social butterfly that loves flitting about a party and engaging everyone in conversation will not last long when paired with a possessive personality. A marathon runner with a driven nature shouldn't commit to a couch potato. A Dachshund and a Great Dane can easily fall in love, but they are going to have a hell of a time making puppies. Some couples are just not a good match no matter how hard they want to work it out or how much you want to please each other. Knowing your own personal ambitions will help you narrow down the man, or breed, that is right for you.

Like a true veterinary technician, I always provide a disclaimer. I am not an animal doctor. I didn't go to medical school to become a veterinarian. I am an LVT. Just like a nurse, LVTs can only relay the diagnosis that a doctor makes. For that reason, I can't tell you the tumor I recommended you get removed off your dog three years ago is a sarcoma, and based on your dog's cough, it has almost certainly metastasized to the lungs. I can't tell you that the kitten you found and are now rubbing on your face definitively has ringworm, even if I know that these things are true. I can only tell you that these things are a very real possibility and suggest to wait for an actual veterinarian to examine and diagnose your pet. I am also not a people doctor. I did not major in psychology and pursue a doctorate. I can't tell you as a professional that your boyfriend is a narcissist with a borderline personality and acute alcoholism, and you are codependent with abandonment issues, even if I am pretty sure these things are also true. I can only hope that you pursue counseling and a diagnosis from a licensed psychologist or psychiatrist.

I would also like to mention that while I think I am hilarious you might not accept all that I say as comedic gold. If you are offended by any of my jokes I am truly sorry. All veterinary technicians have one thing in common: a twisted sense of humor. This dark disposition endures through school where we rack up ten to thirty thousand dollars in debt and then endure a fifty-hour a week externship. We spend the following weeks pulling all-nighters cramming in order to pass state and national boards. When we become an LVT, licensed veterinary technician, we pray we are lucky enough to find a job where we make fifteen dollars an hour. (Are you laughing yet?) Once we finally get a job at a clinic, the majority of daily tasks involve some type feces or other terrible bodily fluid. All of this has earned us the right to make tasteless jokes. We are able to smile despite our dwindling bank accounts by making inappropriate and callous jokes that are also extremely entertaining. These jokes come from a place of sincere love for animals and respect for this field. Do yourself a favor and don't overthink it. We'd love for you to laugh along with us.

If you are reading this book because you are concerned that your issues are more complicated than your friends can grasp, then they are. If you are planning on or hoping to change your life based on the pages of this book, return to the store and get your money back. Put that money towards a therapy session with someone who went to people school. As we'll discuss later, therapy is not only for people who are broken or love to talk about their problems. It is for people who need a little direction on the way to being better. It is for all of us. Every insight into your inner self is worth it. The people who say "therapy is a waste of time" or "therapy doesn't help anything" are the people who waited too late to go.

My ramblings are fun to read and might help you relate to your friends or verbalize your own thoughts and concerns, or they might just make you giggle at what an idiot I was. I am really okay with either of those scenarios. Laughter and the idea of community in times of crisis are a great psychological comfort, but to be clear, you shouldn't use this book as a substitute for a professional's diagnosis. These chapters detail how I have calmed my nerves after a bad day at work or how I reminded myself that I am not perfect when I was upset with a friend. Writing this book has been MY therapy and I'm letting you read the notes.

The stories written are a combination of my life, my family's experiences, stories that I heard, things I saw on TV, and my version of the truth after watching myself and my friends travel through hell and back. Some are factual examples and some are vast exaggerations. To my dearest friends who read chapters and say to yourself "I can't believe she wrote about me!" let me assure you, I didn't. To absolute strangers who read this book and exclaim "I hope my friends don't think this way about me!" please know that they absolutely do. Mine all think these things about me, as well. We all think that we know better than our friends but are rarely forced to cope with one of them writing a book about mistakes we know we have made. Whether you and I are bosom buddies or bitches passing in the night that will never meet, know this. I can honestly say if something I wanted to include happened to only one of you, I didn't write about it. I would never embarrass a strong woman seeking to better themselves by singling them out. Each of these stories happened to no less than two of you. Much more likely it was you, three coworkers, two acquaintances, and then, after spending days or weeks picking up the pieces of all of your lives, I went out and did the same damn thing. Take this moment to find a little solace that you are not alone. You are not special. I am not special. Men are not special. We are all a little bit of stupid, and we all just want a little bit of love. I truly hope you all find it, because I thank God everyday that I did.

When reading this book, remember that a dog might be man's best friend, but you are the one that's going to keep him warm at night. Take notes! Let's get going!

Don't Pet It, Unless You Are Prepared To Keep It.

After years of working in veterinary clinics, I learned that if I chased down and picked up every adorable stray I saw, or took home every animal abandoned at my clinic, I would have a menagerie that could easily rival the San Diego Zoo. I try to be very logical when planning for my next pet. I've spent months walking through shelters, staring at pair after pair of soulful eyes and knowing they weren't the right one for me. Sure, I could have taken him home and learned to love him, but I would have known that we were only together because of my bleeding heart. And it wasn't because I truly believed in the partner I had picked. I would have ended up resenting our union as pet and owner. Nothing this new pet ever did would be right because I would know that we should have never been together in the first place.

Many of those canines you see in the shelter are there because of those exact circumstances.

An owner picked a pooch for any number of reasons, despite knowing better, and broke up with their pet when they realized how poorly things were going. Even someone as prepared as I am at caring for an animal would have been overwhelmed with resentment at only taking a pet home because I felt shamed into it. You can walk away from this situation feeling only guilty frustration at this unwanted responsibility and wishing you were in love.

When beginning to consider the rescuing of some poor creature, human or canine, you need to look at your life and decide if you are ready for such a drastic interruption. You need to prepare yourself and your home. You need to buy food, water bowls, maybe a collar, and definitely some toys. You need to be aware of the motivation behind your decision to share your life and know your expectations. Most importantly, you need to calculate how much work you are willing to put in and what you are willing to give up.

Before you know what you want in a soul mate, you must figure out what you want and expect from yourself. We often forget that we are fifty percent of a relationship. If we are being very honest, even the best relationships with men lean more toward a sixty-forty ratio with women being that sixty percent. It's not fair, but that's the burden of multiple orgasms. By knowing what you bring to the table, you can know what you both expect from one another.

By committing yourself to a longer and more rigorous training schedule, you can enjoy a younger consort and embrace all that youth has to offer. Taking in an older beast might require less training, but you are forced to accept that some chronic bad habits may not be open to change. Sometimes you can teach old dogs new tricks, but you cannot change them. And let us not forget about the grooming issues with the longer haired varieties.

People don't come defined in clear-cut boxes. The majority of us have a hand and foot in a different category, and there are exceptions to every rule. I've seen a lot of my friends and family pursue men, hoping to engage in a long-term relationship without realizing that they probably shouldn't be looking for anything romantic in the first place. They are likely stuck in one of a few "it's complicated" relationship mindsets. Let's look deeper into your situation and investigate if you are happily hyper-independent, desperate, or if you would rather be fostering a pet instead of permanently adopting one.

Are you happily hyper-independent?

Do you barely have time to grocery shop? Are your work hours erratic? Is work hectic and stressful? Do you crave time out with your friends and become exceedingly happy when you get those oh-so-needed margarita nights with the girls? Does the time alone for a bubble bath and clearing your Netflix Queue make you giddy with excitement? Or the opportunity to curl up with an ice-cold, dirty martini and a book teeming with washboard abs, tawdry sex scenes, and no more substance than brain bubblegum seem like the perfect cap to the seventy-hour work week you just finished? Are you single and happy about it?

What's the perfect addition to your chaotic schedule? What can you do to relieve your stress? Get a puppy!

A happily, hyper-independent person is going to have a hard time committing to a long-term relationship. This type of person finds the idea of voluntarily taking on the additional responsibility of another life and emotional baggage absurd. They chuckle under their breath in disbelief that you would make such a horrendous suggestion. That would be ridiculous! Why would you commit to trips home to take a puppy on a walk when your lunch break is already rushed? Who would want to cut short invaluable networking dinners just to spend time preparing evening meals for a whimpering creature?

You might be a workaholic or you could just hold your social life in the utmost importance. You don't want to be tied down by mundane, domestic habits. You travel on a whim. Plans make you cringe. You are a fly-by-the-seat-of-your-pants girl. You would read *Cosmo*, but that rag has nothing on you.

Your inner monologue is screaming, "Why would I subject myself to even later nights when I barely sleep as it is? Why would I commit myself to grocery store trips to stock my pantry with things besides the lean frozen meals, coffee and vodka that fulfill MY needs? Do I really think I am available enough to take on the emotional and physical needs of another being?"

If the thought of taking home a puppy throws your driven, overworked mind into a tizzy, then why would you think you need to take home another person?

If you fall into this category, you know who you are and what you want out of life. You are empowered and self-reliant. You come and go as you please. You have goals, and you aren't quite sure if those include anyone else at this juncture. The greatest obstacle that you are going to encounter when faced with an opportunity to share your life is what you are willing to give up. You will know you aren't ready for that commitment if at this point in your life the answer to that question is nothing.

While society and your mother want you to settle down as soon as possible, you shouldn't need to talk yourself into this. You'll notice earlier I said *happily* hyper-independent. If you are unhappy with your current status, then you should actively work to open yourself up to a relationship. If you believe you are ready for a partner, then you are closer to finding the right one. You may need to start making cuts to how many days a month you travel for work or re-evaluate your hobbies or social standings.

Dollar longneck night is not a hobby. It will not be easy to change your habits, but the right guy will give you a reason to fit into his world, and he will make an effort to fit into yours. You will both work at helping the other, and you will both make compromises. You can become a puzzle piece to fit the other. Compromises are not about one person molding their whole world around another like clay around a rock. They are not about one person staying stiff and rigid (not in the fun way) and the other changing their entire shape. It's about you melding into each other and becoming a new form entirely. While both of you may not always have a smile on your face while you go through these changes, you should always think they are worth it. You should be happy to sacrifice for the one you love.

If right now you are happy, fulfilled, and not destroying property or your health, then why did you buy this book? You didn't. Your friend did. In a year or so when you decide you are not quite so content, you will want to read this book. Right now, do yourself a favor and give it back to the friend who told you that you *have* to read it and stay exactly how you are!

Are you Desperate?

You could be the opposite of our happily hyper-independent person. Not only are you unhappy with where you are in life and blame the lack of a man for this melancholy, but at this point you might be a little bit desperate. Not desperate in the sense that you are dressing pillows in flannel shirts, naming them Brian, and setting them a place at the table, but desperate in the respect that you are *ready*. This next relationship could be *it*. You will make sure that the last time you were a bridesmaid was the last time you will ever be at a wedding without wearing a veil, and you are ever vigilant for *the one*.

The idea of undivided attention is mind-boggling to you. Yes, you are never home, but to love someone who loves you back sounds like a dream. Perhaps, this is what you needed to break your workaholic cycle. You will have a reason to take lunch breaks instead of eating at your desk. You will finally have an interesting conversation to contribute at your next dinner party. You feel like you never have time to meet anyone worthwhile, and when you do get a rare spare moment you feel like you are bored at home waiting for a friend to call you up. You are tired of the same night replaying itself like *Groundhog Day* and only seeing your friends when they are broken up for the next two days with their current on-again-off-again, long-term boyfriend.

You see this as a solution. A new pet will allow you to look forward to coming home instead of dreading being alone in an empty house. You two can go for walks. You can go to the park. You can eat together. You can curl up and watch *Animal Planet* together. You can create a new lifestyle.

This will fix you! All you would have needed was this motivation and a final push to become part of something.

Hear me clearly when I say that a pet will not fix you! A man cannot fix you. Entering into companionship for the wrong reasons will undoubtedly turn out worse than being alone. While something to focus your love and attention on will seem to fulfill you, it is only a distraction. It will merely be a distraction from a job you hate, from the time you spend alone, from the stories your lying friends tell you of their "perfect" partners. You will find that shortly after encounters with your new love interest become less than perfect, every issue you have with yourself will resurface with a vengeance, and it brings friends: regret that you were unable to make yet another relationship work; resentment toward your partner that he wasn't able to make your life better. All the while you have insecurity convincing you that the problem must be you, even if this relationship was doomed from the start.

Whether it is on your own advice, professional help from a licensed therapist, or the unlicensed advice from your most blunt friend, you must learn to be content in your own skin. You have to know that you are strong by yourself in order to contribute effectively to the partnership. Once you are secure with yourself you will find that you are less obsessed with seeking fulfillment from any outside sources. The days when you needed attention from others in order to feel like a success will become fewer. There will continue to be days that you crave companionship, but you will not discount your life when you find it lacking. You will no longer be desperate. You will realize that you do not need the dog you chose. You want him.

You need to know these things before you find your next Mr. Right. No matter what preconceived notions you have right now about how ready you are, how much free time you think you have, once you see those puppy dog eyes staring at only you it is hard to not take that boy home.

Are you too excited about fostering?

Many in this situation seem to lean more toward short-term prospects. You think to yourself, "I'll foster! I'll just keep this little guy for a while, teach him a few tricks, and then he can be placed into a new home." On the outside this seems fantastic. You are able to enjoy all the excitement of a new addition with the knowledge that he will be gone in a few weeks. Your life can continue as normal. Your heart stays safe and hidden. You get all the fun memories and none of the long-term responsibility or pressure.

There is nothing wrong with this option. I am not going to pretend to be a saint. Many, I'm sure, can attest to my past. There are things I wish I had never done but nothing I regret. There are also boys I wish I had never done, but again, none that I regret. The body wants what the body wants and sometimes you will give in to your more carnal desires. Just remember there are leash laws in every state, and you would be wise to put a "collar" on that boy!

As convenient as this fostering option seems, as a long-term situation it is not the healthiest for your body, mind, heart or soul. Subconsciously, I always wondered if this fling would lead to a real relationship. I told myself I was prepared to send them packing but also wondered if we would be the exception to the rule. Bitches always want to be the exception to the rule. They think, "Maybe new guy and I would make it past this fostering stage and have a funny, sexy story about how we met." Truthfully, I was always just a little sad when we didn't last, and I was left convincing myself this was what I had wanted all along.

We had a saying at one of the clinics I worked at concerning the precise time frame for adoption. "Get 'em to the shelter while they are cute!" We would arrive to work on Monday morning to the sight of a cardboard box on our doorstep. This box was usually full of barely weaned kittens or puppies with a note that read something like, "Please take care of them because I can't." Unfortunately, we can't either. Veterinary clinics are not shelters. They are not set up to house litters with immature, weak immune systems in cages next to sick or dying animals without also making these new babies sick as well. Many of these litters were automatically sent to the closest shelter. We did our best to give each one a fighting chance. We would set up these furry, little infants with first vaccines and test them for illnesses on the clinic's dime. The goal was to do anything we could to give the shelter a head start on their adoption process without having to spend any of its own funds.

Occasionally, the staff would rally together and be able to trade off nights to keep the litter at home, or employees would volunteer kennels to house them until they were ready for adoption. We all tried to not get attached although it was virtually impossible. When they had reached an appropriate, healthy age and were ready to officially be adopted out, I had the misfortune of being the bad guy. I would announce to the staff that our furry friends would be leaving at the end of this week so that we could "get'em to the shelter while they're cute!" This usually prompted at least one employee to cry and volunteer to become official owner to their favorite member of the litter.

All of the animals at the shelter are deserving of love, but just like at happy hour, the hard truth is that perky puppies get the most attention and there is a small window when your puppies are their perkiest. Yes, there is someone out there who will love you exactly how you are. True, looks are not the most important thing in a relationship. Yes, you should love yourself including all your flaws, but years of partying in smoky bars are bound to take their toll. Eventually you might want beautiful wedding pictures with a not so aged face, children that will not be mistaken as grandchildren, or have the possibility to travel without having to hike Fuji with a cane. It would be terrible to wake up one day wishing you had not wasted your youth on fleeting men.

To combat the old adage that it is better to have loved and lost, you give away a piece of your heart whenever you add a name to a list of failed fosters. You may not notice at first, but unlike the pride you can feel knowing you found permanent homes for all those furry friends, all you will feel is sadness when you look at the list of men you kept for too short of a time; men who were either unwilling to commit to you, or who you were unwilling to commit to. This sadness only gets worse when coupled with the common phenomenon of these same men getting engaged six months after you stop seeing each other. Believe me when I say it will be well worth the extra days alone to look back and know you limited the number of times you had to reject or be rejected to only the times when it was worth it. You may have to "love yourself" a little more, but at the end of the day you will love yourself a little more.

Every relationship has to fail to get you to the one that will last "until death do you part." You don't need to be shamed by a failed or fun tryst that you knew was heading nowhere, but you don't need to purposely bump up that list either knowing you will be upset when it ends. You don't have to take every stray home. Hold your heart to a higher standard and be proud when you find someone else who does as well.

Picking the Right Breed for You

Who doesn't love seeing the trailer for an upcoming movie with a spunky canine character voiced by an attractive pop star and animated to interact with a different attractive pop star? The answer is anyone in the veterinary field. It isn't that we don't love seeing an adorable Marley steal the hearts of millions in widescreen. We do. We cry right along with the rest of the audience. In fact, we start the waterworks ten minutes before every other sad soul in the seats around us because we see exactly where that last vet visit is going. Oh no, I'm sorry, was that a spoiler? The movie is, like, ten years old. I apologize for nothing.

The pooches most often recognized in our biggest blockbusters include Dalmatians, Golden Retrievers, Border Collies, and Saint Bernards. Every time a producer decides that a breed is *the* breed for this summer's feel-good family flick, veterinary clinics nationwide are inundated with a year's worth of puppies named after a leading character that will soon be a burden on a mother somewhere because little Billy YogaMom has decided he doesn't want a beagle if it doesn't fly or talk. That's actually a true story.

The most famous breeds to use in movies are often the most destructive in our homes, for good reason. Hollywood likes to glorify the worst breeds of dog to own because millennia of selective breeding has given them all of the traits required to endure the rigorous schedule of a movie set. Ask any aspiring model slash actress, "What does it take to make it in Hollywood?" You must be ambitious, determined, eager to try until you achieve that perfect take, and of course food driven. Our popular movie dogs are just that. They are working breeds. They have been bred over generations and generations for a purpose. This purpose was much more important than playing into the movie's tag line. The jobs these dogs were bred to perform were at one point, and in some families still are, vital to the survival of the owner's family. A dog that doesn't protect livestock or isn't able to save a farmer's precious time moving the herd to where they need to go is a detriment to the family's ability to survive a rural life. It is important to know that in an urban environment these dogs thrive on having a job to fulfill all that unused energy. Working dogs aren't happy unless they are utilized to perform a very intense task and they will create their own task to perform if necessary. When suburban families don't have a task to offer, they may notice their border collie or blue heeler has begun herding their children around the house as if they are sheep.

The "purpose" mindset in people is what inspires a bottle blonde from Kansas to convince herself the insurance commercial she is filming is her big break, and it gives her the determination to cry on cue thirty times before the director calls for lunch. This ambitious instinct is what allows a golden retriever to act as a search and rescue dog spending hours following a scent or seeking human life amidst rubble. It also means Goldie will bounce a basketball into a basket thirty times for the price of a Milk-Bone. This same drive is what pushes that same golden retriever, living inside an open concept, ranch-style home in a gated community with only a few ten-minute bathroom breaks throughout the day, the fortitude to chew through dry wall to get to the mailman. They are also equipped to destroy kennels, purses, phones, and school projects for the fun of it.

Many breeds of dog need a regular, exhilarating workout. Many times, establishing an exercise routine with these guys by playing fetch for half an hour or taking them for a brisk walk around the neighborhood will solve your behavioral issues. When an owner comes in with a destructive pet the veterinarian's first questions are about both the owner's and the pet's exercise routine. During these conversations, it is often quite obvious that neither owner nor pet are getting regular workouts.

The same is true for human couples. We need regular exercise and an exhilarating workout. Not that kind of workout, you dirty, little bird. What I am talking about is a stimulated mind. A stimulated body isn't a terrible thing either, but it has a much shorter expiration date when you do not combine it with an interested mind. You need someone to excite you, to fit your lifestyle, to balance you out, and to make you better. When humans lack these common goals with a mate, they can become destructive as well. They may not shred newspapers or destroy couch cushions, but they develop their own damaging habits such as inappropriate flirting, cheating, or chewing through drywall to get to the mailwoman.

You know at least one person mimicking this behavior. You might know someone who presents themselves as the female equivalent of a greyhound: possibly slender and sleek, but absolutely high-strung and extremely neurotic. This neurotic behavior can be presented in different ways. Some withdraw from too much impromptu social interaction. They prefer to be in control of a situation. They like to inform you of how independent they are. You may recognize this friend as one who only wants to participate in plans that are their idea.

Some act rude. You love them and see the wonderful thoughtful things they do once they are established as your friend, but everyone else sees them as a bitch for the first six meetings. I'd like to say that they are subconsciously offensive, but the truth is that sometimes they know exactly what they are saying to people. They are most likely also aware that it was rude. I'm talking blunt in a way that would leave you staring in a mirror debating the shape of your eyebrows for hours. They aren't trying to ruin your life or leave you contemplating the entire contents of your closet. They genuinely think they are helping you by making you want to cry. They just need to make sure you know that you commonly wear a terrible cut of pants for your body type, even if they had only known you a total of seventeen minutes.

Like the steady hand of a nurse and the way a calm veterinarian can make vaccines painless for a panicky dog, a well-matched partner is able to handle your neuroses, as well as make it easier for you to cope with them. When people make a statement about the compatibility of my husband and I, my favorite reply is, "This man knows precisely how to handle my version of crazy." You need someone who is not afraid of you at your worst. You don't need someone to coddle you or order you around. You need someone in the trenches beside you.

I had one friend in particular that embodied the neurotic lifestyle who was not only aware of her rudeness but was proud of it. The first time I visited with her after she had begun dating her newest pack member, she was relaxed and calm, and most surprisingly she was complimentary. She exuded an air of serenity that made every interaction with her a pleasant experience. She was a greyhound with all of that excess energy put to good use during the race and her demeanor now calm and breezy. The obvious reason was that she had finally found a partner who was matching her step for step.

Previously, she had only picked the pretty breeds. The breeds she picked, although very camera ready, were also more content to sit still in a make-up chair for hours. These pets always looked good on paper and as her plus one at a wedding in front of jealous, single bridesmaids she knew from college. However, these beautiful, useless men didn't want to work for her and they didn't expect her to work for them either. I could tell that her new man was giving her a workout. He wasn't afraid to go on a hike or a spontaneous weekend getaway. He knew how to handle her crazy. He allowed her to answer "Are you bringing a sweater to dinner?" with a rambling explanation ranging from the possibility of maybe them being late for dinner since there was a football game in town. Answering questions he hadn't asked such as would they have to take the long way around and cut back through downtown because of construction. Maybe this would cause them to hit more lights and if so, they would need to leave a half hour earlier if they wanted to go to the restaurant she liked and be at the dessert place before all of her favorite flavor of crepes were gone. He would let her talk herself out and then lead her back to the original topic of whether or not she needed outerwear this evening. With this new man she was comfortable. She was content. She had found someone to dissipate the energy from her working breed personality.

Someone who condemns you for your ambitious or neurotic nature isn't *the* someone for you. If you constantly feel anxious or restless, you need to find out if what you are missing is the support of a man that compliments your personality. A good man will want to help you level out your manic phases but will not make you ashamed of them in the process. If you feel like you are walking on eggshells around someone because you are afraid he will not like who you are in your moments of trial and tribulation, ask yourself what his response will be when something truly upsetting happens. If he can't handle you when the drycleaner doesn't have a cardigan ready on time or when the restaurant loses your reservation, will you be able to lean on him in the event of a lost job, miscarriage, or car accident?

Understand your own disposition and what breed of man you need to match that temperament. An active personality requires a counterpoint that also loves activity to be happy, and a languid one requires a mate that isn't going to try to drag them to a damn 5K every other fucking weekend. I mean, shit, Steve! Really?! We can't sleep in on the *one day* I have off this week?! I think I've almost worked through that one. Anyways. I made a joke in the introduction about a Great Dane and a Dachshund falling in love. While two different breeds of dog or conflicting personalities of people will always have the prospect of getting along and even falling in love, in the end they must be able to match each other stride for stride in order to last. If not, these two will find that you are torn. You will Ping-Pong between constant resentment at feeling forced to slow down to accommodate your partner's lethargic pace, or guilt for walking at a speed comfortable to yourself and leaving the other behind. This mismatched gait only heightens that restless and anxious discomfort within your dynamic.

Like my friend found someone to exhaust her outgoing and high-strung character into docile charisma, you have to find someone willing to take you for a walk. Find someone to build you up in your lowest moments. You need someone who wants to throw that basketball into the air forty-seven times so you can wear yourself out hitting it with your nose and aiming for a hoop. You need someone who wants to put in the work, and you deserve someone who will do it with a smile.

Sit Means Sit: Communication

Relationships of any kind require compromise and sacrifice. We all know that, mainly because our girlfriends like to remind us of it. Most commonly, your bosom-buddies will subtly repeat your own advice back to you after a rant about how your companion of choice has ruined another dinner party with incessant whining, but hopefully no accidents on the carpet. Sharing your existence with another being makes you look deeply into the corners of your life. You must prioritize your activities, feelings, and needs; often, when they have never had competition. You are forced to decide between what is important to you and what is important to someone else, and hope that you end up still liking each other afterward.

Communication between you and your significant other, and honesty with yourself about your own expectations, are of key importance. If you need help understanding the importance of communication, I propose a quick fun experiment. I want you to make a sandwich in front of your dog. The best sandwich you can dream up. A sandwich loaded with juicy, thick-cut meat, crispy bacon, imported cheese, and perfectly crunchy lettuce. Slather both slices of whole grain artisan bread with garlic basil mayonnaise. Now, take a big delicious bite of that perfect sandwich. With that exquisite bite of sandwich still in your mouth, try to muster enough movement in your tongue to tell your dog to lie down and roll over, and at the same time try to prevent yourself from spraying bits of half-masticated sandwich onto everything within a two foot radius. Did he sit? Did he roll over? Of course not. He stared at you with excited, intent eyes, pretending to understand you. He seemed to want to obey but was really just wondering if he was going to get a piece of that sandwich. Because he was distracted, the message was unclear to him. Even though you tried to articulate the words you wished to convey, they were not expressed in the way that you would have hoped. He tried but could not comprehend. All you have ended up with are sandwich bits everywhere and a mess you will inevitably be forced to clean up.

When you show up on a date faintly smelling of your most sultry perfume, your hair perfectly coiffed, and a new matching panty and bra set in red lace underneath that little black dress that flows around you and accentuates best what Zumba has given you, you are nothing but a delicious sandwich to a man. Men are going to look at you the same way as their canine counterparts. They will give a terrific effort. They will nod, express interest in what you have to say, continue conversations and deliver innuendos in the most chivalrous way possible, but really they are just wondering when they are going to get a piece of that metaphorical sandwich.

This is why learning what your desires are for a relationship is essential. When we know what we want, we can figure out how to properly convey that to a man with both our words and actions.

As a woman, we can often make leading statements to our mate like "I cleaned the whole house but didn't get to the dishes" followed by "what are you doing on your day off? Maybe I'll make dinner when I get home." We know any other woman will understand that we expected the dishes to be done when we get off work, but it would be idiotic to assume a man thinks like us. We would never dream of speaking with a dog this roundabout way. Not one of us expects a dog to comprehend the logistics of the vacuum and why it is not the enemy. It does no good to communicate with them in a way that they won't understand. "Excuse me, Sparky, dear. I'd love to address your irrational fear of the *Roomba*. I'd be happy to put out the manual for you to peruse and ease your fears." Good luck. Instead, we must think like a man so we can speak to a man. We must speak the words we say as a man would and be crystal clear. "Since I did the laundry, please do the dishes tomorrow on your day off so that I can cook dinner." Or go out to eat as a reward for both of you helping around the house.

As a single person who only has to worry about their own agenda, you may not see the use in spelling out the things that are so evident in your life. Why would you need to remind yourself of all the things you hold most dear? The person who loves you will automatically be aware of your loves and interests and support them so that you never lose your identity. Wrong!

Newsflash, ladies! A man absorbs on average twenty-five percent of the knowledge you present to him, and I'd put money on eighteen of that twenty-five percent as pertaining to you naked. If he has to choose between reminding you to watch your favorite TV show and reminding himself to watch any relevant sports game, it isn't a choice. He has forgotten that your show, or anything else on television, exists. Not because he doesn't care for you, and not because he doesn't love you, but because he really wants to watch the game that's on even if it is mid-season and determines nothing in the playoffs. This is why as women, we must be so adamant about our list of demands and our priority on the DVR. Who else is going to go fetch that ball for us? Your well-intentioned boyfriend is not going to remind you to record this year's Tony Awards.

Whether you find yourself thinking about your need to make a list of terms now, or you recognize the need for a list coming in the future, even as a precaution, you need to think about what you are willing to give up and what you are not. You should let it be known from the beginning that some things are negotiable and some are not. You need to train yourself to communicate these conditions in a non-threatening way. You need to understand that by the time you are pressed up against something fuzzy and warm, you are past the point of "Was this a good idea?" or "I wonder if he is going to mind that I am vegan since he works as a butcher?"

Putting these deal breakers down on paper is a great way to organize your thoughts. Think *Vision Board* meets *Match.com*. Don't shy away because you are concerned that your values and thoughts aren't significant. Don't be afraid to write down the smallest things that mean the most to you. If you need time at the gym without him three times a week, write that down. If you need Sunday mornings alone to drink coffee at a café by yourself because this is when you reflect on your week, write that down. If he has to have a certain religious background, write that down. If he needs to be active in certain parts of your life such as your love of interpretive dance or put your Sunday dinner with your parents above fantasy football, then write it down.

Only if you have a clear understanding of what you expect out of a relationship will you have any hope of communicating those needs and learning where to compromise without caving. Without that explicit communication, you end up negotiating your own priorities and beliefs. Believe it or not, there is a happy medium, and only the two of you can decide what it is. Your friends and family will always be on your side, and therefore, they cannot judge how "fair" a compromise is. Let's go with an example I used earlier: Sunday dinner with your parents.

You begin dating fake boyfriend, Handsome McAwesome, in April. Things between you are sublime. He begins coming to your weekly Sunday dinner with your siblings, significant others, and parents. Still, sublime! Now, it is August or September, or whenever sports happen, and things could very easily take a turn for the worst. Fantasy football starts. Pre-season gets rolling. Before you know it, those dinners that Mr. McAwesome was so eager to make a good impression at are now a nuisance interrupting his Sunday evening of keeping tabs on the weekend scores. How do you react to this?

You could freak out and order Handsome to come to dinner all season. You could tell him he doesn't really love you if he can't make it. This option makes him choose between his friends and you. It will instigate resentment regardless of whether you win or lose this argument, and will set an example of how autumn in your relationship will continue forevermore.

The other equally off-putting option is to roll-over. You could tell him he never has to come to dinner and give him a free pass to ignore you every Sunday. This shows him that you are satisfied taking a backseat to his friends and his fantasy team for the rest of the relationship. It sets a tone for the rest of your time together that his priorities are your priorities, and that's what matters.

While both options may seem like hyperbolic examples, it is what it will feel like to the both of you. If you say he is required to come to dinner, it will feel like you want to take his friends away. If he says he refuses to come, it will feel like he doesn't care about your traditions and your family. I've always said that what we remember are usually not the facts, but how those facts make us feel. While it doesn't diminish my amazing insight into the human spirit, it turns out Maya Angelou said it first: "People will forget what you said, people will forget what you did, but people will never forget how you made them feel." If you both communicate this badly, neither of you may ever forget how this feels. So why not make this small snag in your relationship an example of how you should also solve the big issues? Discuss what you both think is the ideal situation for each of you. For him the solution is football every weekend. For you, the dinner that has become an institution in your week. Now, both of you move. You agree to let him leave right after dinner so he only misses the first quarter of the primetime game. He agrees to miss the games that aren't as important and stay for dessert those nights; as long as if, during playoffs, you accept that he will be MIA. Talk. Find a solution that makes you both comfortable, and also shows the other person that you care about them.

Yes, this sounds over simplified. Yes, this sounds redundant. Yes, this sounds too easy. But if that is true, then why do we all screw it up so badly? Why do we wait until year three when we are living with someone and now are forced to be honest to address the fact that we hate that they watch too much football or play too much Xbox? We shouldn't wait until we are engaged to have the conversation about our faith or religion. We shouldn't wait until we are pregnant to discuss how we want our children raised. Why do we hide who we are and wait until our lives are too intertwined to easily untangle and show our partner who we really are in our core?

I once had a friend who dove into relationships headfirst. She devoted everything she had to making it work. She became friends with his friends so that he never had to be uncomfortable around people he didn't know. She ignored wine night with the girls and instead made dinner for him. She cancelled on Fajita Night and BBQs because his friends were going to a movie. She made his life her whole life. She was the "perfect" girlfriend.

This woman could never understand why the relationships consistently failed at around six months. It was because she set an unrealistic and unhealthy precedent from the beginning. At six months, she felt comfortable that she had secured a man and now wanted to start acting like herself again. She wanted back the wine nights with the friends she had been neglecting and now missed.

Since she had never expressed interested in a girls' night before, it made him insecure that she suddenly wanted time away from him. She wanted to include him in her friends' gatherings and vice versa so she could fully integrate their social lives, but she had made priority of talking to us about him and never discussing us with him. This put him at a disadvantage when they did hang out with her friends. He knew nothing about the person trying to engage him in conversation, while they knew intimate details about him. It made the conversation seem one sided and both parties became uncomfortable. She suggested more activities with her friends instead of his, which made him think she didn't like his friends anymore and became defensive. She wasn't honest in the beginning, and now the relationship they were both invested in was a lie. It caused tension and arguments. It made him seem jealous and controlling, and it made her seem like she was trying to change him. Even though those weren't the facts, it was how they both felt and it was their reality.

Communication is not the enemy. Fear of what that communication will lead to is the enemy. The only solution is to stop being *afraid*. You have to trust that there is a good end to every conversation. Even if it isn't the solution you were hoping for you must have enough faith in yourself to say, "I am worthy of a relationship that builds me up and does not break me down, even in the times I am not right. I am worthy of reciprocal love. I am ready to make someone a priority who works to make me a priority in return."

Behind all well-trained men are patient and hard-working women. You are reading this book as a person who wishes to train a dog would read up on training techniques. You are hoping to teach your next man to roll over on command. Both the dog and the trainer are required to spend time putting in effort. The difference between nagging your pet and communicating the important aspects of your relationships can be a fine line to walk. It is only recommended to train dogs in about five to thirty-minute intervals depending on how many commands you are working on. This is because if you say the same words over and over again for too long, they lose all meaning and the animal loses interest. It proves difficult to give specific advice on the difference between nagging and effectively communicating since each relationship will dictate its own line. A man who says you "nag" him all the time might just be trying to avoid communication. A woman might think she is communicating, but she could just be retaliating passive-aggressively by rehashing topics until she gets the answer she wants. The advice I can give you is if either of you are not getting the answer you want and continue repeating the conversation, then you need to decide if it is the answer you need. If you are wrong, have the courage to admit it. You will be wrong. You will be wrong a lot. He will be wrong a lot more. The only way for you both to understand why you each felt the other was wrong and prevent it in the future is to communicate and be clearly understood.

Everyone communicates differently. Maybe he needs like twenty minutes of quiet time when presented with an issue in order to organize his thoughts and not overreact, yell or make things worse. Maybe you are going to cry whether you are sad or not. He might think that if he is able to make you laugh then the fight is over. You might explain yourself better in writing. Find a way to make it work. Find a way to take the best ways you both speak to each other and set a precedent that will improve any situation for the both of you. Do not let the fight get swept under the rug. It will begin to rot under there. Get this stuff in the open where it can breathe. If you don't fix a problem now, you will have to deal with it again soon, and you will be more begrudging with each return to an unsolved problem.

From the beginning, be you. Be straightforward and simple. Learn what commands work, and repeat the same commands over and over again, to him and yourself. Sit means SIT!

Some Dogs Will Hump Anything In Sight.

It is common in the veterinary world for technicians to have to explain happenings of a delicate nature to clients. At some point a client very similar to eighty-nine-year-old Ms. Franklin will come into the clinic for an exam with her unneutered, overweight, adult, male schnauzer, Fritz. At that time, it is the job of the veterinary professional to describe to Ms. Franklin in detail why there is a vast possibility that Fritz may never stop humping her new leather couch and knock-off Hermes silk throw pillows, even if they decide to now get him neutered. We must explain that when it comes to her precious little Fritz, there is a difference between a learned behavior that becomes a habit and a hormonally influenced one. The difference between these two causes for the same action is the reason her precious baby, who is now twelve years old and defiling her couch, may never stop this, even if you remove the hormones.

A hormonally influenced behavior is most easily understood by reminiscing on the time you spent in high school. You are a seventeen-year-old senior who has finally gotten her braces off and is just a few days from being acne free. You stop at your locker after third period. As you are about to finish the combination on your lock, that boy from your fifth period government class, the one with the blonde, purposefully shaggy hair, comes up to you. Not only do you forget the last number of your combo, you forget that you even have a locker... or hands. He leans again the locker next to yours, pushes those blonde locks out of his eyes and asks how you did on the mid-term. You blush, stammer, and inadvertently play with your necklace until it is a tangled mess. Just as the bell is about to ring to remind you that you are in school and should already be in Calculus, he asks you to prom. You are very aware of your hands sweating in ways they never have, and before you can even mutter yes, you are already making mental plans to jump his bones at a sleazy hotel room after the dance. You are young, and your hormones are in charge of every synapse your brain emits.

As you grow older that hormonal influence fades... for the most part. You learn to weigh options and consequences, and to make informed decisions. You learn through experience that you are able to restrain your urges and not go bounding after everything with a fluffy tail. You start to notice when that guy in the bar with the perfect hair and chiseled abs visible through a distressed T-shirt pronounces it "supposebly". Instead of not caring and taking him home later anyways, you accept the free drink and make an excuse to head to the pool tables without him. You can already see that there is no future here, despite how tan he is and how good he will make you look at your high school reunion. You begin to occupy your time with men who are in pursuit of a career. You leave behind men who are satisfied with employment as head fro-yo cashier and only interested in beating the cover charge at any terrible chain bar with any terrible cover band.

Some men will never care if a woman knows when it is appropriate to use your or you're. They will only care that she has a great rack. Some men, much like an unneutered dog, will never reach a stage where they acknowledge and take responsibility for their actions. Not that they can't learn. Unlike a pooch that is unable to stop himself from expressing his affection for your new throw pillows, a man can learn. A man can choose to be neutered. I don't intend the term neutered to be viewed as one that is derogatory or emasculating to men. I use this term to describe a man that makes a conscious decision to ignore hormonal, impulsive decisions. An unneutered dog will dig out of a yard in search of anything to occupy their time. They feel no loyalty to their owner waiting at home. An unneutered dog is a player.

Read this carefully, ladies. A man can choose to put aside his most basic instincts and truly commit to one woman. He can choose monogamy or living together or marriage or whatever the common goal is between the two of you. A man can even make the choice to abstain from sex until your comfort level has been met. It's true! He can choose to or he can choose not to. And yes, it is a choice.

Contrary to the opinion of some men and women, men are not sex hungry heathens out to rape and pillage. Sex is not a physical requirement, even for the most bro of all the bros. Your girlfriend is not a personal sex toy. Fucking is not an obligation. If your boyfriend threatens to cheat because you are not letting him express himself physically, or if you think that if you don't fuck him that he will find someone to cheat with, that doesn't make him "just another guy". It makes him a prick. It makes him a cheating prick, and you shouldn't want to date him anyways. I can tell you the best sex you can possibly have is when you feel connected. That connection doesn't come with pressure or force. It doesn't come from guilt or fear of loss. It comes with trust. I can't imagine any of the men I know being happy with the accusation that they are capable of such deplorable behavior. Men should be offended by this opinion and actively work to disprove it.

The poor pet that is now my husband, the same man that inspired this book and also hates the title, agreed to do just that. After some weeks of intense dating and the constant tension of whether or not tonight was the night, I faced that issue head on. The last thing I wanted was to lose him. I was twenty-three and could already tell that I was going to fall hard. But I also didn't want to have to continually see the let down in his eyes every time I said stop. He was a gentleman, but he was also twenty-four. There's only so much expectation and disappointment a guy can take night after night. I told him I wanted to wait until we had been an officially exclusive couple for three months before we crossed too much of a physical line. My plan with this conversation was to push him over one of a few edges. We would learn that we were looking for different things, and figure out if we were both willing to work for something worth more than a casual fling, or at least to give him the dream of a decided finish line.

Whether or not I made it to my own declared deadline is irrelevant in this context. Let's just say I failed by a long shot, but the little fella didn't know I was going to cave when I did. He let me dictate my comfort level. He could have pretended to be okay with it and never called me back. He could have said that he wasn't willing to wait and obviously I would have had to call it quits before I got too deep. Either of those options would have been understandable for a man that just wants to act like a dog.

Instead, he made the choice to see what we could become. He made the choice to accept an offer into a more committed relationship. He made the choice to consciously ignore his more sensual instincts and, for lack of a better analogy, sit and stay. I am so glad he did, and I'm so glad I did, too.

Not all dogs are going to choose to stick around. Some will always choose to run the streets looking for any bitch in heat. And why would you want them to stay if they are just going to pout and growl about it? You don't want to be with someone who doesn't truly see you as the be-all end-all of his or her dating forays. All of the effort you could put in would never be enough. You will never teach a dog that isn't neutered to stop humping everything in sight. As fun as a bone can be it isn't worth the dog attached.

Men Want Meat; Dogs Want Bones.

"Don't worry. Real men want a little meat. Only dogs want bones." My mother told me this saying once when I was a teenager as I stood staring into the mirror scrutinizing every ounce that wanted to lap over the waistband of my jeans. She then giggled and issued twelve more jokes about how terrible men were before making plans to go drink at Chili's. I think back at myself at nineteen. If only I could be as thin now as I thought I was fat then. Just for one day. You idiot child, so unappreciative of your young metabolism! Sorry, I'll focus.

As soon as I heard this saying it captivated me. It spoke to me in a profound way. I was chubby and a bit awkward for the majority of my younger years. There was a small break in my early twenties where I was on a liquid diet of vodka and cranberry that my BMI said I was "healthy". I was crying all the time due to the bushel of men that inspired this book so my abs were banging! Apart from this break when I was unaware of how thin and adorable I was, my chubby self-conscious phase lasted through my late teen years and into my early twenties... Mid twenties... Late twenties. *Fine*! I'm still fairly awkward and depending on the time of the month, I fluctuate between mildly chubby to fully bloated. To give you some perspective on my perpetual chubbiness I trained intensely for seven months to run a marathon, sometimes running up to fifty miles in the span of just one week. I ran all 26.2 miles of the Houston Marathon and upon crossing the finish line I was still chubby and awkward.

After feeling overweight and under-attractive for the majority of my life, this saying that "real men wanted meat" was empowering to me. It told me that it was okay for me to look the way I looked. It told me that just because a guy wasn't interested in me didn't mean I needed to change, as long as I was happy. But I wasn't happy with myself for a long time. I suffered through bouts of bulimia and depression and blamed my body for what I see now as a control issue. It took way too much alcohol and devoting myself to a work out routine (even if intermittent) to make me feel confident about my body. I will never be the one hundred and nineteen pounds I was in college but that's mostly because I'm keeping my food down now. Frankly, I've become way too cheap to waste food I'm paying for. I'm proud now of my chubby body and everything it has achieved. I still struggle with feeling attractive which is why even now I repeat this adage to myself when I have a rough week and am unable to go to the gym or when I just really, really want that extra martini and dessert with my salad. Thank God I have found a man that makes me feel beautiful every day. He has no problem telling me when I classically lay the trap of "does my ass look fat in these jeans?" that they do look a little tight. He, of course, blames it on the dryer. Where this type of honesty would have sent Past-Mallary into a shame spiral, I accept now that he loves me and wants to be honest when I ask him a question. He never makes me feel anything less than gorgeous, and as much as I appreciate that, if I didn't have a base of self-worth developed for myself already I would not be able to believe his compliments. If you can't believe yourself when you say "There is beauty in me," then you will never believe anyone else telling you that.

Let me include that this is not a tirade against any specific body type. I encourage everyone to look in the mirror and love what he or she sees. I understand this is unlikely. On my best days as a size eight to ten, and also on the best days of my size zero friends, we both still see that little roll of fat on the top part of our backs that folds oh so elegantly over our bra straps. We both have days we feel beautiful and days that we compare ourselves to a busted tube of biscuits. If you ignore those little annoyances and still strut that butt on half of your bad days, you love your body more than most. That is something a lot of women aspire to and something to be proud of.

This is not about how thin girls are more desirable, or how voluptuous girls are better in bed. It's not about how blondes have more fun or redheads are crazy. This chapter is about loving who you are and finding a man who does the same... Although, personally, I find the most attractive women in the world are about five-foot-two brunette, a little curvy, and named Mallary.

Understand that if you can't be expected to be a swimsuit model then you must know you can't set your expectations to finding a perfect *GQ* specimen of a man either. Sure, we'd all love to come home to Ryan Gosling whispering his best "Hey Girl" line, or Channing Tatum asking us to critique the new dance moves he is preparing for *Magic Mike 7: The Buns Are Back*, but that's probably not going to happen. By all means, don't stop believing. Maybe Mr. Gosling's motorcycle will breakdown as he travels cross-country doing role research. However, maybe you should be a little more reasonable when you are scanning the bar while you eat at TGI Friday's in Podunk, Texas, on a Wednesday and pursue a conversation with the regular guy who smiled at you before you rule him out.

We all have certain aspirations for the one person we wish to commit to. I am a firm believer that attraction is an important part of any relationship. There always needs to be something that draws you to another person whether it is a physical attribute or shared interests, but do not confuse being attracted to someone for lust. While they overlap in some aspects like a Venn diagram, lust and attraction are distinctly different. We are all aware of Lust. Lust is all encompassing and all physical. It is an uncontrollable wanting to touch someone, and once you do it glues your hand to his skin. Lust wipes your mind of consequences until it has quenched its thirst. Attraction is different. Attraction is closing your eyes and being interested in what they are saying. It is not completely devoid of physicality, but it is not reliant on it either. It is the idea that you are equally concerned with whether or not he will kiss you at the end of the night, and also what his credit score is or how much equity he has built in his downtown loft. When in doubt about whether you are feeling lust or attraction, remind yourself: Lust doesn't give a shit about credit scores.

Be careful to not blacklist a guy for lack of lust at first sight. Go on that date! I mean, girl gotta eat. Attraction can grow. When you think about the people you currently find yourself attracted to, chances are that there is at least one person in that group of gorgeous men that you have known for years. In the beginning, you ruled them out because you did not initially lust after them. Now that you know them, you see all of the qualities they have always possessed that you should have paid attention to back then. Remember that this new guy that you are not instantly turned on by after a two-minute conversation, had the balls to ask you out. He might be the kind of person that needs more time to wow you than the time it took to self-consciously flirt in a crowded room. He might be one who engrosses you in conversation you find so intriguing that you just can't help but fall a little into like with him. You should give yourself the chance to see that.

If you outright do not want to go, then don't go. You don't want to feel cornered or forced to attend because that attitude will ruin any small amount of potential this date had. First dates are embarrassing enough without an edict to enjoy them. But if you are on the fence, wondering whether or not to go, then you should go. That one date can give you the information you need. You can find out enough about him in that first date to make a decision about the second. And, duh, you'll get a free meal. Plus, if you don't get a free meal that will decidedly rule out any further dates.

I also think that everyone has a type. We all have a style of person or a particular charm that drives us crazy. For me, my type is a tall, kind of honky, thin, athletic, white guy. But I have learned to not be bound to that type as is evidenced by my five-foot-nine Hispanic husband who broke his foot playing basketball- alone. When you hold fast to only dating people over five-foot-eleven with blonde hair and green eyes, you eliminate everyone at the Greek Festival, and who doesn't love John Stamos? Not only is that mindset extremely limiting but remember that your body will change. The aging process is a guarantee. The death rate is one hundred percent. You will have babies. His hairline will recede. Your eyesight will dwindle and you will need glasses. He will get a beer gut. Do you want to build a relationship based on looks or feelings?

I am aware in this body-shaming-cross-fit generation that the fight against aging is very real. I am not talking about being content to watch the person you love slip into gluttony and sloth while engorging their body with trans-fats and processed carbs. I'm not talking about giving up on health. I am talking about giving in to age. As much as you fight it, you will age. As much as you Botox, your face will look older. As much as he lifts, bro, he will become weaker in time. Accept this. Learn to love a person and not a shell.

The important thing to realize is that when a man isn't into you, it doesn't mean there is a problem with either of you. He is not automatically a dick because he doesn't want to date you. You are not a troll because he doesn't want to date you. It just means that for one reason or another, many of which have nothing to do with you, the two of you are not meant to be. Now, I won't lie. When a guy didn't call me back in my twenties, I am convinced it was solely because of one of two scenarios. One, he was currently in a coma after suffering from a horrific accident occurring on his way home from our first date where he was rescuing a small child from the way of a speeding train and I should move on. He wouldn't want me to put my life on hold grieving for him, because he's a classy guy like that. Or two, he discovered that he was gay immediately after dropping me off as he understood that if he couldn't love me, he must not be attracted to women. Both of those things happen a lot more than you realize. At least twelve men from my early twenties are currently somewhere in comas or gay. And I just have to accept that these things happen.

More often than comas or changes in sexual attraction, a date doesn't work because the two of you simply didn't click. It might be because his ex called him before or after your date and despite you being charming, he is distracted, and therefore you are forgotten. It might be because he has no interest in your hobbies. As happens more often than any other scenario, it is almost exclusively because it was only an average date and why would we expect a guy to waste time on average when we don't ourselves. The difference in an average date and an amazing date is as simple as alchemy. It is magic and cannot be predicted or engineered. Enjoy it when it happens, and don't stress when it doesn't. You can't fake it. So don't try.

When a date goes badly or love doesn't pan out we have to step aside from blaming our bodies. Honestly, your personality might be the issue. Maybe you are a raging bitch. Maybe you are condescending and rude. I'm obviously joking. Kidding aside, I'm almost positive you are fantastic. Even if you were a horrible person, it does not mean you are ugly. You are not too fat. Your boobs are not too flat or too small. You are loveable even on your most unattractive days. There is beauty in you. People around you see it every day. They see it in your generosity and kindness. Friends, family, and strangers see it in a thousand ways that have nothing to do with your looks. If you don't recognize that and embrace the confidence that being loveable brings, then how is anyone else supposed to?

Look in the mirror today. Instead of focusing on all the parts of yourself that you hate, focus on just one that you love. Find just one. Start with one thing that you love about yourself, and then you can constructively grow to love the other parts if you can and accept the ones you can't. If you hate that you have chicken legs start doing squats. If you hate that your hair is wavy, binge watch YouTube videos and learn how to straighten like a professional. Your physical appearance has nothing to do with your worth. Appearance can be adjusted and changed. It will change on it's own without any help, so help it in one-way or another. You can help it by accepting it and no longer condemning yourself for it. You can help it by taking steps to move forward and change it. As long as you sit idly by and do nothing to change a body or lifestyle you despise you will only feel more helpless. If you are not working toward something you have no right to bitch about it. If you are happy, don't change. But if you aren't happy, you are only going to grow your unhappiness by becoming complacent.

Learn to love what is inside. It is the only part of you that does not age. It grows, and the only way it grows is by being fed by love and confidence. See yourself everyday as your dog does. Feed the inner you by accepting yourself or accepting the challenge to grow with change.

Even Dogs You Don't Own Will Still Try To Pee All Over You ... I Mean, Mark Their Territory.

The amount of urine a normal healthy male dog is capable of producing is astounding. If you have ever questioned this, take a pup to a strange dog's habitat. That can be anywhere: a dog park, a human park, a neighbor's backyard, or the lobbies of a veterinary clinic where you can watch an unhappy receptionist clean up your dog's mess. As a guest in this new domain your pet will waste no time in beginning to traipse over grass or tile sniffing out all of the very best places to alleviate their suddenly engorged bladder. They will urinate themselves into a dangerous level of dehydration, it seems, to make sure they cover any scent markers the "reigning" canine has laid out.

Men seem to do this as well. Men will make it evident they don't want you but they sure as hell don't want anyone else to have you either. Despite this, they want anyone who looks at you to know that someone else was there first. I experienced this most prominently in my life after having very recently entered into my latest serious relationship. I had finally met that guy that you instantly like. The like grows into love, and you are just waiting for him to say it first. In those fantastic instances, it's like all the mutts from your past know you've found one that is purebred. I was getting asked out constantly. Female dogs will emit a pheromone when in heat. Males can smell it for about a mile around which is why the males that impregnate your dog are often from a few neighborhoods away. I am quite certain that when a woman is happy in a new relationship she emits something very similar, and every ex of hers knows to start texting or calling.

I had never been one to get asked out on a regular basis. I was not accustomed to being chased. I always seemed to fall into that friend with a ponytail category from eighties movies, only there was no Blane waiting *Pretty in Pink* style for me with a birthday cake. *Ever*.

It felt good to suddenly be an object of desire. It is nice to be wanted. It's the reason women take dates they know are going to lead nowhere. It is the reason we answer calls from our ex's, or text back assholes that have girlfriends just to tell them we aren't interested and engage them in a conversation that will last the rest of the night. As rewarding as dignity can be it is validating to have someone want us.

During this time of being pursued by any guy who had yet to be neutered, a previous foster pet of mine called me up to "innocently" have dinner. Where this particular foster was concerned sometimes these dinners were truly those, just dinner. We would talk, and he would inevitably be more charming than most of the men who were actually trying to date me. We would say goodbye, kiss on the cheek, and head home. Sometimes the evenings consisted of dinner and then a very tantalizing dessert back at his place or car. Not knowing which this would be, I first declined explaining that I was currently in a loving, exclusive relationship, and nothing was going to happen between him and me tonight. Then I went to dinner anyways. Partly because I was naïve and truly believed we could be just friends, partly because I had nothing else to do since my new boy was at work, and mostly because I was flattered and it felt good to be wanted by someone.

This guy that I was planning a venture out with was one of the most charming pieces of shit I have ever known. Understand that when I say piece of shit, I say it with a big ol' smile on my face. He was adorable, sexy, and he smiled with a crooked smile that let you know that whatever was being planned for the evening was not just going to be a very bad idea. It would also be addition to very memorable. He was the kind of guy that make it seem like him cheating on his girlfriend with you was your idea, but also pulled a Sweet-N-Low for you every time the waitress refilled your glass of tea because he always remembered just how you took it. He once ordered the dessert I had mentioned on a previous date while I had excused myself to the powder room to surprise me. It's hard to turn down that kind of personal attention to detail when he tells you he respects your new relationship.

Arriving at his house, we exchanged pleasantries, and I was given a tour of the house he had just purchased. Guess where it ended? If you guessed the bedroom, you would be right. Even the twenty-three year old floozy that I was knew how terribly cliché this was. In all honesty, if I had thought the man that I had started dating, the man that is now my husband, was any less terrific I would have leaned in when my foster pet tried to kiss me. But I didn't lean in. I was tired of playing games. I knew this for certain as soon as his lips got within four inches of mine.

After shooting him down we both laughed off this failed advance and continued the evening. We had dinner and a drink, or three, and we talked about the guy I was dating, the girls he was seeing. In those sexually charged conversations, the man I was fantasizing about was not this man at my table. It was my boyfriend who I was daydreaming about. The topics continued at dinner, each time establishing in my mind just how much I liked the man I had chosen whom was waiting to meet me when he got off work, and reminding me how lucky I was to never have fallen in love with the man at my table.

Dinner ended. We drove back to his house, and he walked me to my car. He opened my door for me, of course, as a true gentleman does. As I was putting on my jacket to leave, he leaned in again...

The fact that this foster pet knew I was crazy about my new boyfriend was irrelevant. He was ready to intervene in what he saw as a challenge to his territory just to prove to him that he still could. Did he want to date me and only me? No. Would he have easily ignored the fact that he was dating someone else if I had agreed to have sex? *For sure!* There is not a doubt in my mind. To him, it was just sex. Guys find it easier to distinguish sex from other emotions. Men are better at separating like and lust. They are very aware the difference and rarely have an attack of conscious about it. Think Ryan Gosling's character in *The Notebook*. Although still hopelessly in love with Allie, he still shared a bed with war widow, Martha Shaw. Martha knew what she was getting into and still fell in some version of love with him, but she knew that they both needed the companionship. Now, imagine all that ceremony minus all actual feeling and class.

As a dating woman you need to be able to decipher whether he is seeking sex or love, and whether you are as well. I always recommend true unfaltering love before you opt for a roll in the hay, but this is the twenty-first century. You and I would be naive to think that we want to date every man that makes our lady parts tingle. There will be many men in your life that will make you reconsider your once strong stance on not fucking a Starbucks barista. You are an adult and are able to decide on your own whether you are emotionally stable enough to enjoy a little bit of free love, but I would advise against it. Not because it wouldn't be all you imagined sex in a storeroom on bags of whole unroasted coffee beans to be. Not because it wouldn't be satisfying or fun, but because you aren't in love. Sex is hands down always better when you are in love. Do you want to be in love or do you want to get laid?

Men always want to get laid. In the way women always want to fall in love but look forward to great sex, men are the opposite. To men, love is the surprise at the bottom of the cereal box. They are really excited when they find it, but they were going to fuck the cereal anyways. I mean, eat. They were going to eat the cereal anyways. Anything they find at the bottom is just a bonus. Listen to this next line very carefully. Just because he wants to have sex with you does not mean he wants to enter into anything more serious. In biblical times to say something twice served as a way to emphasize the importance of it. So I'm going to say this again because it is quite possibly the most important thing a single woman can ever learn. Just because he wants to have sex with you does not mean he wants to date you.

We always hear that anyone can say they love you but their actions are worth a thousand words. But we've also been screwed over by someone who acted like they loved us when they were with us.

We need to combine the words they are saying with the actions they are taking to get a full picture. If a man tells you he doesn't want a girlfriend right now but he can't deny how much he likes you, and then he leans in for a kiss, what are you to focus on: his actions which say he wants to date you, or his words which say he doesn't? We will want to focus on the one that makes us feel the prettiest which is usually the kiss, but that's exactly what you need to be careful of. I always recommend putting the majority of stock on the option that will put your heart in the safest ground. We tend to swoon and make excuses for him. He just got his heart broken. His job is really stressful. He wants to date me, but the timing is wrong. What he is really saying is he wants to have sex with you but not date you. We must be careful to recognize this and guard our hearts accordingly. I am sadly too familiar with allowing myself to become part of non-relationships with men who didn't want to date me but couldn't let me go. In the end they always say the same thing. "I told you from the beginning that I didn't want a girlfriend." So who should get blamed for my broken heart in this scenario?

He is right. He warned me, and I failed to listen. That doesn't exonerate his behavior or give him a free pass in the part he played destroying my planet but when it comes down to it, he can only ruin the parts of my life that I let him into. I accepted the move he made on me. I chose to ignore the signs, and I let him in. I am ultimately to blame for the hurt that I now feel. Do not let someone into your life that doesn't care if he is there or not. If you could be any other girl to him, then let him be with any other girl. You are worth so much more than being convenient. Being aware of who you should avoid when getting into a relationship doesn't mean you will never get hurt, and it doesn't mean that you should always blame yourself for the sadness you feel when a relationship ends. It does mean that you might have a more rational view of breakups and be able to learn more from them.

While we tend to see it displayed more often in the male population, men are not the only gender capable of this behavior. Let's take a look at how we as females can also exhibit this behavior of wanting a relationship but holding yourself back from one hundred percent commitment.

Perhaps you want to be peed on but are resisting. Strike that. Allow me to rephrase. Maybe you are deeply committed to a relationship that is everything you want it to be, but old habits keep creeping into your lifestyle. Chico, my rescued hobbled Chihuahua, was adopted when he was upwards of eight years old. Young still for the lifespan of a small dog, but he had been an outside dog for the entire length of this. After a lifetime of marking his yard when, where, and how he wanted, a change in routine was difficult to accept. He transitioned well into an inside dog and became comfortable sleeping on an orthopedic mattress instead of dirt. He still growls when it thunders, but I imagine he's happy to be out of the rain. He did well with every part of this conversion into inside life with one exception. He likes to relieve himself on anything new. Should we return from a trip and not immediately unpack our luggage, he will immediately urinate on it. If we purchase a new piece of furniture, pee. If we move a piece of established furniture, pee. Chico is resisting.

How are you resisting? Are you still flirting with more intent than is acceptable? Are you keeping secrets? Are you refusing to commit? Are you cheating? If you are holding on to a part of your former single self, perhaps, it is because you are indulging in some aspect of your past. These bad habits are satisfying a part of you that your current relationship is not. Figuring out what this missing piece is will be critical to your success. You cannot carry on living a double life. You aren't Wonder Woman. At some point it will catch up with you if you continue to live in the duality of single versus committed. It will usually catch up with you and bite you in the ass in the "I got busted sending an inappropriate text" way, which will not end well. Figure out what you are craving from this previous life and work to introduce it into your current world. Continuing to keep secrets or act on impulses is comparative to a guy who is faced with a commitment ultimatum saying, "I just have a lot going on right now, but I don't want to lose you". You are keeping a part of yourself just for you. Until you can entirely commit your whole self you will run the risk of losing everything you have because you aren't giving it all you've got.

Dogs live in a world of convenience. Food on the floor is fair game. Toys appear out of nowhere. They always have somewhere to sleep that is warm and a person to snuggle with; and while they may have a preference of whom that snuggle buddy is, in a pinch, anyone will do.

Men are not supposed to live in that world. Dogs do. Boys might. Men don't. Men will work for what they want. Men will show you they do have a preference. If you are what they prefer, they will show you that you are worth working for.

A Kennel Is Not Jail, And Neither Is Marriage.

I was once a person who swore that marriage was for the birds, or dogs, for the sake of the theme of this book. Remember that part about what is real and what we feel? Well, I felt like I was the late-blooming, ugly-duckling product of a woman who constantly spoke of how disposable men were supposed to be, which I now recognize as a defense mechanism. I felt like my father was a man who was a hopeless romantic, meaning he consumed himself with the wrong type of relationships, but never quite got it right. In reality, they were amazing parents who always did the best they could for my brother and me. They made sure to get along and not bash each other in front of us. They had their flaws *cough-mom-dad-nudge-nudge-wink-wink*, but we never worried. We were extremely loved. As happens about fifty percent of the time, they divorced one another and other people after that.

I grew older and entered into a series of high school and college relationships that consisted of me being in love with men who did not love me back. They thought it reasonable to keep me in the role of pseudo-girlfriend, and I allowed myself to be kept in that role until they let me go because they were ready for a "real" girlfriend, a real girlfriend that wasn't me. A large piece of my heart resigned to never wearing a white dress, and I convinced myself that this resignation was a choice. Instead of acknowledging that it was based on sadness that I would never be enough to satisfy someone, I convinced myself that this choice was based on fear of divorce. This fear was rooted so deeply that the first time I inadvertently verbalized a wedding comment I had a panic attack and began to hyperventilate.

I remember clearly the Sunday routine that my mother and I had when I moved back home after college. We would do the dishes and fold laundry, and watch an entire day of wedding TV brought to you by TLC and your biological clock. My mom watched to get ideas for my sister and I, while I tuned in to watch spoiled catty women scream obscenities at the man they tricked into proposing.

This tradition continued into the time I was dating my husband, Gabe. So there I am, terrycloth towel in hand, half paying attention as my mother swooned at the ivory dress on screen. My starry eyed mother, lost in imagining me in a veil, asked me if I wanted a big or small wedding. Without conscious thought, I responded. I was just finishing rattling off a vision of a larger wedding due to the size of Gabe's family, most of whom I hadn't even met, as the icy hands of fear gripped my lungs and made it impossible to breathe. I sat on the couch and choked, exhaling deeply into my folded hands. I realized that if it was to Gabe then maybe I did want to get married, if it was Gabe. A panic attack is the best way to realize that your priorities have changed.

If you don't want to get married, more power to you. After that story, hopefully you understand that I get it at least a little. You are a grown woman and can make your own decisions about the path your life should take without being lead on a leash, unless you are into that. It's totally cool if you don't want to get married. In that case, you can really substitute the word marriage with long-term committed relationship. I know you want one of those two things otherwise you wouldn't be reading this book.

I ended up getting married, and I am never regretful of my choice. I love my husband more than anyone or anything on this planet, but I can see the viewpoint quite clearly of those who would reject this idea of legally binding monogamy. My advice is to never close yourself off to any opportunity. Never cave on your principals but don't be afraid to change them either. You might be right. You may never want to get married, but you may meet someone who changes your mind and it would be a shame to miss out on that based on leftover principles from a single life lived long ago.

A lot of people have a skewed view of marriage, whether from divorce or bad boyfriends or any combination of our own insecurities. Just like marriage, a lot of people have a terrible view of kennels. It makes it a perfect analogy, really. People see a kennel as jail. All they imagine is confinement, and little sad jailbird puppies wearing stripes and banging an empty food bowl against prison bars. At the clinic we have people beg us to let them know how to salvage the devastation that is taking over their house. They then adamantly refuse to put their dog in a kennel even though we offer this as our most reliable option. These dogs are destroying houses. They are causing damage that makes it impossible to have company and unthinkable that the owner would be able to leave the house. They have essentially made the owner a prisoner in their home. These dogs and owners supposedly love each other. Yet, one is refusing to ask for what they really need, and one is going to continue to do whatever they want because they have never been told to stop. These same owners return to us weeks later to ask yet again how they can regain their house, and eventually the only answer a frustrated receptionist can give is to start using the kennel, get rid of the dog, or agree to be miserable.

If your man is acting like he doesn't want to get married and this is wrecking your world ask yourself if you have been clear. Like a dog that is destroying the house because he has never been told that you want him in the kennel, maybe your mate has no idea that you see this relationship heading toward marriage because you have never clearly had the talk that you really want to be his wife. We always wait so long to have this discussion that by the time we wondering why things aren't moving forward we are almost incapable of having the conversation at all. We get anxious and realize that we are so invested in the relationship that we are too scared to lose it if the conversation goes the way we fear it will. We don't want to know the truth at this point so we settle for what could be a lie. It might not be a lie, but we have to have the talk to know! That creates quite a predicament for a scared little bitch.

In relationships, both the man and woman should be in that kennel together and they should both enter willingly. Not due to threats or yelling or bribes or puppies, but because both know that marriage to this person will be a safe place. Have you ever seen a kennel trained dog? They take naps in there with the door open. It is a place to savor those little treats that are too special for the living room. They take cover in it during storms. It is a safe haven away from the parts of the world that don't make you feel your best. What else would you want your marriage to be?

It is true that, even in the most successful marriages, there are times we do not want to be there. We will cry to get out. We will lean against the bars and see how far we can bend them. We will even bolt from it given the open opportunity. The times you feel this way are the times when you try to remember all those times that this kennel, or marriage, has made you better and safer, and you remind yourself to think of its confines lovingly.

The only time I ever argue with a woman's fallen view of marriage is when she begins repeating her boyfriend's tripe about them only needing a piece of paper in order to validate their love for everyone else's benefit, or defends refusing to get married so the government can't keep tabs on them. It is just an extension of the "I need to express my love physically" conversation we all experienced at least once. There are some men that like to think that a woman who has the priority of getting married is clingy and obsessed, that she just wants to trap him. In canine terms, she wants him to "kennel up".

If you do want him to kennel up, then embrace it. Own it. You are a woman who wants a husband. Welcome to the club. There are a lot of us.

My experience has taught me that if a woman expresses an interest in a long-term relationship, and a man is not interested, he will run fast enough to leave a cartoon cloud of man-shaped dust. He might hang around enough to make you regret discussing ending this charade. He will ask you why you want to ruin something so good, or why you are making an issue out of something so far in the future. You must stand your ground, and tell yourself and him that you are worthy of an exclusive relationship with verbal expressions and forever plans.

So why shy away? If you are afraid he is going to leave, don't you want him to leave now? If you have dreams of white picket fences and 2.5 children with a minimum number of fathers, then you should chase them. You shouldn't let someone else talk you out of it. You choose your future and whom it is with; and you choose when to pursue or change that plan. When you choose to have a rational conversation it may lead to an answer you don't want. This option of an unwanted answer at an earlier stage in the relationship is preferable to living a sad life waiting until you are forced to have the conversation. By then you will have wasted more and more time on a man that didn't want to marry you five years ago and still doesn't want to today.

Like anyone in need of an inspirational quote, I turned to Pinterest. When you read what pops up after typing "heart versus mind" in the search engine there was a quote that struck me with its simplicity. I have never seen the movie Finding Forester, so I have zero idea about its actual context. Hopefully the scene this is from is uplifting and positive and not spoken by a mobster or cartoon dog. The line goes, "Write the first draft with your heart. Rewrite with your mind."

What a beautiful thought. It is such an important doctrine to believe that we can take a situation that our hearts have put us in, such as settling for a relationship not heading where we want it to go, and rewrite our lives using our brains to change decisions based what we know is actually the smartest move. We are not bound by the choices we have already made. There is always hope for a better outcome. It might take time and tough conversations, but you can decide to end your obsession with roaming the streets and find someone to kennel up with.

Some People Should Be Spayed.

A female dog can go into heat every six months for the vast majority of their lives. They can have a litter of up to fourteen puppies every time. An interesting tidbit of information is they can have fourteen different fathers for each of those fourteen puppies. Shortly after they finish their heat cycles, they are very susceptible to an illness we see in veterinary clinics called a pyometra. Stick with me for a very gross but very brief synopsis of what this is. I promise to use the least offensive words I can think of since I know that most people don't want to hear about anatomic horror stories. A pyometra occurs when a female dog isn't spayed. Her little uterus becomes infected, typically a few weeks after she has finished a heat cycle, even if she was not bred. We see this uterus swell with infection to four and five times its normal size.

Some of our patients are young and this situation is following their first or second heat. Their owners never wanted puppies and had every intention of spaying little momma, but due to timing or financial issues, they hadn't scheduled it as of yet.

Sometimes they are adult dogs. They have had a few years of previous litters or heats with no complications. For our dogs that have had successful litters it is especially unfortunate since they are great with their little fur children and now they are almost certain to never have a litter again.

More often, though, our pyometra patients are old. As a matter of fact they are old enough that the idea of this dog having a litter is laughable. They have never had a litter. The owners have no current plans to breed their pet, nor did they ever make plans in the past to breed their pet. They have never been under any financial constraints that caused a delay in this vital part of pet care. It is a shame but these attentive clients are at our clinic within hours of symptoms and our barely sick pooch tends to have a great prognosis after surgery.

Should an owner be less attentive we can see these elderly canines get very sick. An infection in a uterus can cause severe systemic changes, meaning the whole body suffers. The illness makes their puppies not want to eat or drink. This means they can become detrimentally dehydrated. The infection will make its way into the bloodstream, and the patient becomes septic. The liver and kidneys are damaged, sometimes permanently. Treatment of your very ill female pooch requires hospitalization, intravenous fluids, massive amounts of antibiotics, and, of course, taking care of the root of the problem: removing this engorged unused uterus by spaying your dog! It is common practice for the technicians to take bets on how much that swollen, rejected uterus weighs. In some cases, even with diligent treatment and attentive owners, the illness is too much for our poor little non-mommies and they pass away. It is a terrible thing to lose a pet over something so easily prevented.

The cause behind the majority of our pyometra cases is that when little FiFi was a young puppy, Ms. YogaMom was unsure about whether or not to breed FiFi. As FiFi became an adolescent puppy, Ms. YogaMom thought to herself that having to take care of and find homes for a litter of puppies was not a great idea. Since everything was fine with FiFi, Ms. YogaMom didn't feel the need to take any permanent action, in case she changed her mind. She did not change her mind and it became more and more evident that the YogaMom family was never going to let FiFi have puppies. It became such a normal thought in the house that they were never going to let FiFi enjoy the company of a mate that no one thought to have any additional conversations about this situation. There were no consequences up to this point, eliminating any pressure to address the matter. These owners are now walking away from a clinic with a recovering pet and a twelve hundred dollar bill because no one thought it was an important conversation.

Just like that disgusting infection can build slowly in your pet's system a big problem can form underneath the surface of your relationship when the idea of children is not discussed. Not to discriminate between male and female or straight or homosexual, but this feeling will begin within the more domestic person in your coupling as their biological clock begins to tick. I have known many men, with whom I quickly broke up, that had definite plans to have children early in life. I hesitate to assign this blame to one gender role, but within your partnership there will undoubtedly be one person that is looking forward to tying themselves down to play dates and picture books. The other one is looking forward to being tied down and taking pictures. It will do you well to know whom is whom.

As you develop into an adult, you start to look at the calendar as a test each month. Do you want to pass or want to fail this test? The fun part about this question is that a pass for one woman and a fail for another can actually be the same outcome. Maybe you don't know yet if you want an A or an F this month.

I distinctly remember a time when I kept no less than three pregnancy tests in my bathroom closet at all times. The thought of conceiving was such a terrifying idea that it comforted me to enjoy the reassurance of a negative pregnancy test at regular intervals. There were times when I knew the test would be negative but still felt better seeing that single line. There were other times when the agony of those three minutes was my personal equivalent of waterboarding. My twenty-something friends would find out about this routine of mine. They loved to ask me what I would do if the test were positive. I should clarify that they loved to ask me this question once. One is the number of times my friends, who were vocal about wanting children, were interested in hearing me say that should the test be positive I would "cry tears of sadness because [my] life would be over".

There was a period in my life, which lasted much longer than it should have, when my friends would call and say, "I'm pregnant". My gut instinct was to reply, "I'm so sorry. What are you going to do?" I would remind myself that my friends and I are adults now. Some of us are having babies on purpose. I was no longer in an age bracket where a baby was automatically an unplanned or life-altering surprise. I needed to start acting like it. Trust me, people don't like when you instinctually scream a stank-faced "Why?" to them saying they want five children over five years in the middle of a baby shower. Most of my friends were making a deliberate decision to have a child, and I was making a conscious decision not to. Both were acceptable, but a condemnatory response on my part in regards to their choice to have a child was no better than one on their side to my opposite choice.

Eventually, my feelings may change and being eight days late may no longer be depressing. It will be still terrifying, but I begin to feel hopeful about the future and even a little disappointed now when I do start my period. I still don't want a child right now, and I don't feel the least bit guilty about that. But until I make a more permanent decision either way, I am making it a priority to have that tough conversation and make preventative choices.

Some dogs don't need puppies. Some need to be spayed. I am a bitch that needed spaying; at least for the time being, that is. Luckily we are humans, not dogs. We do not have to have a hysterectomy or get our "tubes tied" if we are unsure about whether we want children right now. We are smart enough to know that the pull-out method is not a regularly accepted form of birth control. We have the luxury of contraceptives like condoms and the pill. We also have the mental capacity and opposable thumbs to fully take advantage of these beautiful marvels of modern science. We are fortunate enough to forgo a permanent decision like spaying in exchange for a temporary solution like making that dog wear a collar.

My husband and I have had quite a few of these tough conversations. The first was when we were deciding if our futures were going to align as we both reached the age that you stop casually dating and contemplate buying a ring. If you are planning on staying together for the rest of your lives, you need to decide whether the two of you will be relying on children to take care of the both of you in your old age or if you are betting on well-invested book money to pay for that retirement villa in Venice.

We approached the subject again after being married for a short time when my insurance changed, and there was going to be a two-month lapse in my birth control pills that was to precede a drastic increase in price. After being off my birth control pills for three weeks I felt better than I could ever remember for the first time in ten years. We discussed all of our what-ifs. What if I got pregnant? What if we spent the money each month and how it would change our budget? How do I feel being off artificial hormones for the first time in a decade? We concluded that with some creative math and proper planning we would most likely be able to avoid a baby, and either way it would be worth the risk to save some money and keep my body a little healthier.

Most recently, we had a discussion when he overheard me from the other room talking to the TV and my dog about what a cool idea I thought adoption was. Another when we decided to theoretically have one child and adopt one.

We continue to have these conversations to make sure our paths are always aligned. They are scary, and I usually tear up from nervousness but they are worth it. We want to make sure neither of us will end up resenting the other from lack of information or the other's true desires. If I had always dreamed of a full house, and he was dead-set on only one child, it was important to know ahead of time. If I never want to push a child out of my vagina, and he feels the biological need to keep having children until he produces a male heir, we needed to know.

Now, I'm not thinking that this needs to be a first date conversation. Admittedly, I do have a dear friend who enjoyed a fanciful first date in which her and her now husband discussed their future together through the next ten years. Impressively, they have lived up to most of the expectations they set for themselves that first evening. My thoughts, however, are that most men probably just want to stick to conversational topics such as where you want to eat dinner and how you liked the movie you just came from. It is best to accept that this dear friend of mine is the exception, and any other guy who acquiesces to this topic in the first three hours of dating is likely stalker material. The ideal time to make your honest intentions known about your preference on babies is around the time where, should this conversation go very badly, it hurts enough to know this relationship had real potential. Don't wait so long that a few wine weekends won't take care of that disappointing aftermath.

Just like a pyometra is preventable, so is the hurt felt from calling off a relationship that should have been spayed much earlier. Do you want to be spayed or do you want to be bred? Do you even know yet? There is no time limit on when you need to make that decision, so don't rush it. There are definitely biological factors for a person that wants to parent genetic offspring, but there are also options like adoption, surrogacy, and fertility treatments that can give you the extra time you need. It is better to be mistaken as your baby's grandmother instead of their mommy than to have a child before you are ready. If you think you need a little more insight on this matter, whom should you seek out for information on this very specific topic?

I can tell you there are a few people to definitely not discuss your fertility with. You should never rely on the advice of your overly maternal friend, your Ke$ha friend, or anyone related to you in a familial or professional manner.

Don't ask your friends who feel it is their destiny to be a mother. There are friends of yours that already have children and friends that are already planning for the children they have not conceived yet. Both of these sets of friends are constantly organizing their imaginary play date calendars and are excited to add you to the roster. If you ask them their opinion, they are very biased. They tend to vote yes regardless of additional information like how you still haven't been to Europe or how you are absolutely not ready. These motherly women know how happy motherhood has made them. They are excited that you might choose this path, as well.

Likewise, don't ask your Ke$ha friend. You know who this friend is if you have one. If you live in Houston there is a good chance that for a portion of your life up until very recently, and even occasionally now, I was your Ke$ha friend. The parts of last night that your Ke$ha friend remembers inhibit her from envisioning days that don't include happy hour. She was out very late last night. She will be out very late tonight. A vague cloud of vodka emanating from her pores constantly surrounds her. She is going to tell you that you have plenty of time, and that you should totally wait so that she still has someone to call for a hangover brunch.

I would also advise against asking your mother, future grandmothers, or aunts. Shy away from current bosses no matter how casual the relationship and friends who are birth aficionados, such as midwives or doulas. These people all love you. They all want the best for you. But like everyone, will subconsciously have an agenda that is all their own. People always give positive recommendations based on how much it will affect them. You having a baby will mean a new grandbaby, showers and parties, and getting to purchase adorable clothes for you. Other than that, your having a baby will have very little effect on their everyday lives.

Should you be in a relationship and internally debating whether you have, need, or want the baby bug you should really only be talking to one person. The one person you should be talking to is the person who will be promoting you from a bitch in heat to full-fledged mommy. As influential as your friends and family can be, they aren't the one knocking you up. They aren't going to be holding your hair back when your morning sickness hits at three am. They aren't going to rub your feet when they swell too large to squeeze into your Converse, and they aren't going to be the one in the delivery room with you wishing to the Lord above that they had stayed on the northern side of the curtain. Granted, your potential future father may not plan on doing these things either, which is the reason you need to have the conversation with him.

Discuss all things that you would be dishing out with your friends with your mate. I can tell you whether my friend wants her son circumcised. I know what names she plans to let her husband decide between. I know what religion, what pre-school, what color the nursery will be. Does her husband know all of those things? He should! You are making *the* biggest decision you will ever make. You are making the decision to tie yourself to this person in a bond that divorce cannot remove. You are making the decision to commit the rest of your life to a child, and take on the role of mother for as long as you live. You are going to have a *baby! A fucking baby!* Talk about that and treat it like it is a *huge* deal, because it is!

And then once you have made the decision to try for a litter, buy my other book "How to Train a Baby". Kidding... sort of. We'll see how this one sells.

On some level, you know what you think you want but that doesn't mean it can't change from a no to a yes or vice versa. Be prepared for it to change. Be prepared for that change to be inspired by a person that makes you daydream about a baby that has your eyes and his smile. And, in the name of all things holy, pray that it has a smaller head than you did in those baby pictures you found of yourself.

He Has To Love Your Pack.

I had worked as a kennel attendant, receptionist, technician, and supervisor in clinics for ten years before I took a stray animal home to become one of my own. In veterinary terms, that might as well have been a century. Most employees get coerced into bringing abandoned or found pets home on a bi-monthly or, at longest, a yearly basis. I held out longer than virtually every single person in my profession. The first pet I ever took home from a vet clinic was Chico, the Chihuahua. Chico was a hit by a car and came in with obvious signs of poor upkeep, if not outright neglect, and was abandoned. The owner "needed to run an errand that will only take about thirty minutes" and decided to never return. At that point, I was not worried. I felt certain that my resolve would hold and someone else would take responsibility for this sad furry soul.

Most people are not aware that when a pet is left to become the property of the clinic, there is a lengthy process to allow the clinic legal rights to the pet. The transfer of ownership following abandonment is at its absolute fastest a two-week process. Poor little Chico was left to sit in a cage with a crushed pelvis and broken spirit. Legally, all we could do was make him comfortable at the clinic's expense. Since the owner only authorized charges for one dose of pain meds and radiographs before he left, every additional dose of pain medication, meals, bath, and treatment to rid this fellow of the thousands of fleas making him miserable, were completed at our clinic's cost. Yes, we could have racked up a bill under the owner's account, but we were well aware we were not getting paid for even the authorized charges. Calls made to the owner were unanswered. Certified letters were returned from an address that did not exist.

Chico sat in a cage for weeks getting pain medication and all the yummy food he could eat. The staff took turns providing companionship in doses small enough to prevent any one of us from getting attached considering his prognosis. He was unable to walk on his rear legs. He could shift from side to side, trying to reach a level of comfort to alleviate the feeling of grating bone on bone, but couldn't stand. Out of fear that he would hurt himself further in moving and dragging his mangled rear end. He was kept in the smallest kennel in our boarding facility. He could not have been happier. He's the only dog that I have ever thought had a constant expression of gratitude. For possibly the first time in his life, he got a bath and was free of fleas. He slept inside on the cushiest pillow we could find which I imagine was quite a step up from his backyard life with a bed of dirt. With the extent of his injuries, we never expected him to walk again, and to be quite frank, we wanted what we all expected to be the last days of his life to be as contented as possible while the legal countdown continued.

Approximately four days before Chico's clock struck midnight, the little bastard got a lucky break in the form of a slow week in the clinic. No surgeries and no appointments allowed for an afternoon of wandering the halls looking for something to clean. What do you do in day practice when you want to avoid cleaning? You provide "enrichment" time with the boarders, meaning you play with all the puppies.

It was a beautiful autumn day in Houston. For those unlucky enough to live outside of Texas that translates into it was the solitary day of September that is less than ninety degrees. After purposefully avoiding the little termite for three weeks, lest I get attached, I decided to take my turn spending time with Chico. I gingerly sat Chico in the sun allowing him to enjoy the grass beneath his paws what I thought would be for the last time.

So there we sat. Chico sat feeling the rays upon his face, eyes closed leaning into the breeze, and me, a few feet away, leaning against the chain link fence. I watched him almost smile into the warmth of the sun, and mentally forced myself to push him into the "this is for the best" and "at least he had one more happy hour out of a kennel" portion of my rational veterinary brain. That's when the little fucker stood up.

It is alarming to simultaneously feel four different emotions at once: proud of an animal's progress, annoyed that you put yourself in a position to become enamored with a dog you don't need, worried that you can no longer in good conscience allow all the plans that made so much sense an hour ago to be carried out, and defeated because you know you are going to take this guy home. I think I muttered out loud in my annoyance, "Good for you, ya little shit".

I did not need another dog. I already had two dogs, a full time job, a fixer-up house we had recently bought, and a new husband who loved animals but was not as enthralled with the idea of so many of them as I was. A Chihuahua, of all breeds, was the last thing I needed. The stereotype of snapping Cujo-like Chihuahuas is not entirely untrue. Many technicians will gladly choose to take a temperature on a pit bull over a Chihuahua because our sweet pibbles are much less likely to be aggressive than the snarling ankle-biter charging me as I try to offer up a treat. As I put Chico back in his kennel and trudged down the hall to find our doctor and inform him of my new plan for our patient, I made a list of rules in my head. My husband must be on board. He comes first. Chico must get along with my other dogs. They come second. He must not be a biter. I cannot, in good conscience as a member of the veterinary profession and a member of a household, have a dog that actively bites.

I tell this sad and inanely long story to bring up a point. I have a pack. My pack includes my husband and my dogs. They are the most important things in my world, and I would be lying if I made it out to be anything else. We have a hierarchy in our pack. We have a pack leader. My husband lets everyone else think that is me. Truthfully, I love and respect that it is he and not I. That is another chapter. Literally. I had a whole life that had nothing to do with this new member I was looking to add. It was important to me that I understood my priorities, and important to my pack that I respected them enough to show them that I trusted in our hierarchy. As much as it saddened me to think about this addition not working out, I was fully prepared to give that boney little Chihuahua back to the clinic and let the chips fall where they may for him. It wouldn't have been fair to my pack to watch their "leader" ignore their opinions, play favorites with the new guy, and put us all in harm's way just because I was following an infatuation with a plucky new friend that just happened to stand up.

You have a pack too. You have a group of people who are imperative to your survival. This can be your emotional, monetary, social, or familial survival. My pack was a husband and a few dogs. If you are single, your pack is your friends. They are a group of people that you need to understand the reason behind your choices and support them, whether they are excited about them or not. Your pack is not supposed to make or break your decisions, but when you call to talk to them about the new guy, you trust these people to give you advice that is in your best interest and the best interest of the pack. If Chico had been aggressive and a danger to the pack, he would not have been allowed to stay for fear he would hurt another member. If your guy is a danger to the pack then your friends are not going to want him around for fear that he is going to snap.

If you are in a functioning pack, that's amazing. Congratulations. You understand the give and take that is so important in any relationship and especially with your friends. But what if you aren't a functioning pack? Are you a danger to your pack? Or is your pack a danger to you? Is your pack against you or are you working against the pack? If you think there is a problem then it has to be one of these options. If you feel like you are always in a situation where your pack is nipping at your heels, let's figure out why. Either you are constantly bringing home a dog that bites, or you are in a pack of bitches.

Some friendships that start out like a summer movie sequence can become dysfunctional after time through no fault of yours or theirs. Maybe they are friendships you developed at a young age, and the adults you have become are too different to be compatible. Maybe you became friends simply because of proximity and convenience, as will happen often with co-workers of a similar age or your friend's mates. Regardless of fault, in order to fix the dysfunctional dynamics you must first identify them. By finding and attempting to fix these concerns, you could rejuvenate the friendship and avoid having to eliminate these friends. It can be difficult to decide whether it is you, your pack, or your pack leader that creates the problem. In my experience, I have found a few key points that will help you figure out who is the saboteur.

If it is you, you will notice a few things about the dynamic of you and your friends when dealing with potential mates. Think back to your past three relationships. For each of these relationships try to remember when you and your friends had a "How are things going, just kidding, we know they are terrible, let's drink wine" night. When you had one of these sacred nights and you were venting to your pack about how you just don't know how to make things better, was it hard to remember which of these nights were which guy? Probably so. Because the problem with each of your relationships is always so similar, it may be hard to differentiate between evenings. You have a type, and that type is pretty destructive. You are always in the same situations with the same type of guy.

If you think this is starting to sound familiar, move to step two of the "oh, God, it *is* me" timeline. If you can narrow it down, can you think of three pack conversations about the same guy? And can you put them in chronological order? Think about what your friends' words of wisdom looked like.

Did it seem to become increasingly more frustrating for them to repeat the same things? Did they add an additional glass of wine with each talk? Maybe as the conversations progressed phrasing became more blunt and attempted to lead you down a more definitive path. You were apt to be upset at their honesty during that last visit. You were very likely to plan on ignoring their advice and then ignoring them for about a week. Don't worry. They anticipate you ignoring them. It's the reason when you excuse yourself from girls' night early in a defensive mess they let you leave. They take this time to discuss how many concerns they have about you and your new mate.

Please, don't be offended by this exclusion. This is our own little way to even the score, because we know we cannot win. We need this time to be on the same page. During this time we will question ourselves. Were we too harsh? Are we overreacting? Should we really be this concerned? We use this time to discuss our own motives. If I am taking out my own frustrations on you, then I owe you an apology, and the rest of the group will tell me that. We don't want to be too demanding or too harsh. We want to do the best for you, and we need this time to make sure that's what we are doing.

Of course, we also discuss you specifically. After a spat like this, you will avoid us for a few days and then often come to speak to each of us individually or at least text one of us off the group message. This one extra glass of wine without you is a way for us to all to come to consensus. The more you hear advice, the more you absorb from it. The more you hear the same advice, the more you think there is something to it and the more you will recognize the parts of our opinion that you agree with, or the parts you don't. We want to make sure we are all on the same page and that if you come to any one of us, we are giving you similar guidance.

If this sounds like a recurring theme, it's you.

So what do you do now? You are in love with someone who probably isn't the best for you. You feel like your friends think you are stupid for repeatedly choosing this breed of man. You are stressing out that your type is terrible for you, which you are now thinking probably stems back to something rooted in your childhood that you should definitely address with a licensed therapist. You feel like all of this information is all crashing down upon you. All these things are true.

Your friends don't expect you to suddenly kick your current pet to the curb just because you have realized that he has the personality of contagious mange, but you know that it would make their hearts a little happier to hear that you did. What they do expect from you is that you start acting like you realize there is an issue. If you express to them that you had a revelation about your actions and then ignore that completely and continue exactly on the path you are on, you are not only showing your friends that you don't care that you are hurting yourself and them, you are also lying to your partner.

Start standing up for yourself. You need to start cataloging your priorities and having open communication with your pack and your partner. You can start slow, but the important part is to start. Hopefully you can salvage all of these relationships and put them on a better path. There may be resistance but that's why you start slow. You don't have to have the answers all at once. You aren't going to turn around and walk through a rainbow while bluebirds sing *Zip-A-Dee-Doo-Dah*, but you are going change one thing tomorrow and deal with the consequences and conversations that result from it. You are going to change one more thing a few days after that, this time with slightly more confidence. You are going to continue doing this day by day with more and more confidence. You are going to slowly become the person that you would want to be in a relationship with and end up with a mate who knows how lucky they are to have you.

So, what if it isn't you? When you are in productive fellowship with other bitches, their job is to build you up, not break you down. There are times I was not a good example of this. For example, there were times when I was too honest and I hurt feelings, or times I didn't realize I was being a bad friend through my own ignorance. Despite this, I never intentionally broke up a couple or was ever happy to make a friend feel like a failure. I showed up to anniversary celebrations, and smiled as I took pictures with their mate whom I didn't think appreciated my friend. I supported my friend, and there were times that meant supporting a man I did not think would ever be good enough for her. I did it and I would do it again. You should do it, too.

Choosing a new boy toy over the pack is the worst way to show your friends you care about them, but your friend choosing to purposefully undermine your attempts at mating for life is deplorable, even if the mate you have chosen is scum. The reasons they might act like this are many. The motives could be anything from jealousy at your happiness, to their fear of losing their friend, or sadness at your shifting priorities. While your instincts will tell you to respond to this kind of selfish behavior by brandishing giant middle fingers bedazzled with glittering nail polish directly into her face, you would wise to understand the reason this is happening if you hope to save this friendship.

How do you break the pattern of a pack that is getting in the way of you growing a healthy relationship? Meet with your pack and open the lines of communication. Understand you will be walking into a wolves' den. You will be challenging the pack's way of being. Even if it is a crappy way of being, it is the way your pack operates, and they may be scared to change. There is more than a small chance that your pack leader is not going to be thrilled. Take the risk. You need to be confident in your defiance of the norm. No change is ever easy but all things that you believe in are worth it.

I learned in my early twenties that a friendship that cannot stand through disagreements is not a friendship. There are always those that will insist their way of thinking is the only way. At the time I didn't recognize why, but I knew I wasn't meant to live in a box that someone else drew on the ground. My pack was becoming complicated, and it had been that way for months. Each complication centered around one person. I knew that as much as I loved the friend, who had come to think of herself as our pack leader, I was becoming secretive and nervous around her. I felt her judgment of my choices when she spoke to me, and learned that she had begun speaking about me to the others in a less than uplifting manner. I felt manipulated when I tried to express any opinion and she shot me down. I felt ashamed of myself for letting this other person dictate my feelings and my life. I hated that I felt I needed to be someone or something different when I was around her. I was not going to put up with a my-way or the highway dictatorship and I didn't.

I reached the end of my rope. When I discussed this with the other members of my pack it turned out, as it does so often, that I was not alone. It can be exhausting to throw energy at a rubber wall. Nothing sticks, and all that effort is wasted. Our goal was to realign the leadership of our group. Just because a person can't be the leader doesn't mean they still can't be in the pack. We just needed a change. We tried to collectively make things better and work through a power shift since we were no longer happy with our leadership, but once the power was taken away, this friend left, not entirely of their own accord.

Ten years later, I still am a member of the same pack. Our pack works now. We tend to rotate our leadership. We have learned, as we got older, that each of us have our particular strengths, and we now allow the pack leader to be whomever it needs to be at any individual time. I think this has worked best for us. You should find what works for you.

There are two important takeaways from this. The first is to support your pack when a member of them is involved with someone you don't like. Your friend loves you. They also love their mate. This can be very polarizing for them, and they need to know that they are not going to lose you. I have also learned that you will not win. We will go into more detail during our Euthanasia conversation in a few chapters but to sum it up in its simplest form, your friend doesn't need to worry that you are going to leave them. You shouldn't coddle them but don't berate them either. Learn to support your friend. Learn to support her mate. Elevating your opinion of him even when you don't want to will do more to make her feel at ease with you than any half-hearted advice or support you could blubber.

The second is for those pack members *in* the crappy relationship. You know your friends are aware of the problems that you are experiencing, and you may feel that they are ganging up on you at every turn. What you may not realize is how much time they spend worrying about you. Cut them some slack. They spend days debating a call or planning the next conversation they are going to get to have with you. They are worried that if they phrase it wrong that you might spend an extra day not talking to them when the conversation takes its inevitable turn to how you and him are doing. They rewrite texts to speak the perfect supportive line. They spend hours in your relationship, in addition to the effort that their own requires. When they say the wrong thing, try to hear the love behind it.

Support your pack, and let them support you. You both need each other. Remember that.

You must be or have a pack leader (read that like Cesar Milian for full effect)

Dogs love to push their limits. A house trained dog will sneak off to urinate on your new rug or an older dog with zero destructive tendencies will suddenly decide to chew up your video game controller. It is a never-ending battle. We work our tails off to train bad habits out of our pets, and then as soon as we think our job is done, they find a weak spot in the system and punish us for our complacency. It is very much the raptor in the pen at Jurassic Park type of situation. They are testing us.

They don't behave like this because they hate us, or because they are bad dogs. They do so because dogs are instinctively pack animals. They look to you as their pack leader for direction and guidance, and when you are not looking, they seek to take matters into their own paws. Having a dog that does not perceive you as the pack leader can create a severe behavioral situation in your house with ramifications from a few chewed pillows to dangerous aggression.

Having a clear hierarchy in your house means a lot less conflict on your end and a lot less confusion on the dog's end. One of our biggest recommendations to help a dog learn hierarchy in the house is to make them work for food. Sit, stay, or shake. The key is to make them do any physical activity that will allow your pet to realize "I have to do what this person says so I can eat." Eating translates into happy, and you become the reason. When a family is concerned about how a child and a dog will interact we advocate for the child to feed the pet. Children mean eating. Eating means happy. These small things are all done to ease confusion in the household by letting your pet clearly know who the pack leader is. I am no pack leader. Maybe you are. If so, I'll get to you in just a bit. But like foreplay, let's focus on me for a minute.

As a young little bitch, I spent my formative dating years chewing up boys and spitting them out, or swallowing depending on how good of a boy he was that day. I owe so many nice guys so many apologies. I speedily shuffled the nicest of guys into the friend zone. The slightly less nice but still way too acquiescent guys endured a worse fate. Since they were unclear with me about their leadership qualities, I drove them away with acts of deplorable behavior trying to prove to them that I needed a leader.

What I knew at the time was that these nice guys were letting me do whatever I wanted. Oh, and I did. Once I knew that Newbie was a nice guy begging to be walked all over, I certainly did just that. I would return home after making out with someone else at a party that I hadn't invited Newbie to, or even told him about, and confessed to them my true actions. These poor pets instantly forgave me, and I instantly lost all respect for them. They were letting me lead the pack, and I was a terrible leader. I was selfish and promiscuous, and mostly just young and stupid.

What I know now is that I am somewhat, while not entirely, a traditionalist when it comes to what most people view as outdated gender roles. I don't think women need to be barefoot and pregnant. I am not a proponent of us doing all the dishes and laundry while our bread winning husband drinks a beer, smokes a cigar, and waits for dinner to be served on a plate I make for him while my own plate gets cold. I don't believe we deserve to make less money for the same job, although if you buy me dinner, hold my door open, and call me sweetheart we can discuss me making a quarter less. Put your phone down, feminists. You don't need to email anyone. I'm kidding.

All joking aside, what I mean is that I have learned that I do best when my man is a pack leader. I crave respectful authority in a relationship. I need parameters. I need my partner to be clear about their expectations as I am clear about mine, and I very much need him to call me out when I push my boundaries. I don't need an S&M-Christian-Grey-style of control, but I do need limitations. I thrive on them. I like to make my husband a plate at dinner even though he would never expect me to. I like for my husband to take care of the yard, maintain the cars, and to take the trash out because I think it's icky. I have no problem hopping on a riding lawnmower and pretending it is a go-kart with a shredder attachment, and I am very capable of killing a roach. But I want my man to do the edging and fix a fence, and I want him to pick up said dead roach because what if it comes back to life in the tissue.

Even people close to me are often surprised when they make a comment on me being the head of the household, and I quickly correct them with the actual dynamics of my home. One of the stories I tell most often about my husband is one in which I pushed my boundaries and he promptly let me know that he was not going to let me treat him like crap. We were on our way to dinner reservations. I had been very late coming home from work and Gabe was barely on time picking me up. The entire day had been a disaster that neither started with Gabe nor had been in any way his fault, but that wasn't going to stop me from making him feel the wrath of what I had been through in the past twelve hours. I was attempting to put on makeup in a bouncing car in Houston traffic and Gabe was attempting to put a smile on my resting bitch face. We were both failing.

In a last ditch effort to salvage not only the car ride, but also the evening as a whole, Gabe made a joke about a bicyclist in the next lane. It was as simple as a comment about how much better he would look in spandex than our bicyclist friend. I am not quite sure of the words I used to respond but they were dripping with contempt. You'd have thought my poor man was skeet shooting with how fast I shot his feeble words out of the air. I sat back in my chair and continued to smear eye shadow as close to my eyelid as possible when the radio was fiercely powered off, and the car slowed to a crawl in the middle of a lane. We were not at a stoplight. Cars were honking and swerving around us. Gabe turned on the hazard lights signaling the cars behind us to speed around our stationary vehicle. I turned to find Gabe looking at me with an expression that can only be described as desperate control and he spoke very calmly when he said, "I know this day has not gone the way you hoped. I'm sorry for that. It's not your fault, but it's not mine either. So I'm going to turn the radio back on, and you are going to not talk to me again until you can be nice, because I don't deserve to be spoken to like this." And with that, he reached over and turned the radio back on. He took his foot off the brake and began to drive the car. I hit the button to dismiss the hazard lights. I looked at him, and all I could say was "I'm sorry."

He was right. Gabe had never and would never dream of using the words or tone that I was currently directing at him towards me. I deserved a lot worse than a composed check to my pride in reply. It could have easily escalated to a full on argument if he had even thought about returning my impetuous tone. That moment that he returned my selfishness with calm authority has become the cornerstone for any disagreement we have had since then. That moment that I was thinking of only myself, and he thought of the both of us is the reason we are such a functional couple now. That is the moment when I fell in love with him. It is when I knew he could handle my crazy. We don't always agree. We don't always get along, and you bet your ass when he is wrong I let him know. We are always respectful. Should one of us try to not be respectful, whether out of fear or anger or just pure selfishness, we have a precedent of not allowing or returning that behavior.

My more "feminist" friends accuse me of setting back the movement. To them, the story I just told is not one of respect but one of me ignoring my true feelings and of a man telling me how to act. No one burns bras anymore because Victoria's Secret charges too much, but I tend to get disapproving stares when I tell new friends I need to let my husband know I am going to plan a girls' night, or I let him order my food for me at a restaurant. I think the assumption is that he is going to deny me friends or is picking a salad off the menu and forcing me to eat it. The truth is that instead of ruining an evening he may have planned for us and we could have shared together, leaving him sitting at home alone. I tell him I am planning girls' night so that he can plan something with his friends, giving us both an occasion to go out as individuals. The waiter only sees a man ordering for me. The waiter doesn't see that, before his approach, my husband isn't ignoring me for the game on the big screen, huddling with his friends, or his allowing his phone to absorb his attention while at the table. He is engaging me in conversation while we wait for our waiter, which gives him the chance to ask what I have chosen before the waiter comes and then he can relay that message. It's a very old world chivalry that I have expressed to him that I prefer, not one forced upon me.

I don't understand other women being seemingly maddened by my actions in the name of "feminism". It was a movement that was created to empower us. Feminism, as I have understood its role in my life, is supposed to be about a woman's ability to choose the path that is right for her. It is about not having that path limited by men, social standings or prejudice, or most importantly, the opinions of other women. It's about the option of choosing who and what turns me on and pursing my own sexual security. Feminism means a woman has the option of being president or CEO. It even means that they can choose to be a stay at home mom or woman who likes to make her husband a dinner plate. Say what you'd like about my predilections, but I have a degree. I am licensed and boarded with the state for my profession. I am mandated to complete continuing education hours each year. I have served in multiple supervisor positions, and at the time I wrote this book, was the sole manager of a multi-million dollar, nine-doctor emergency specialty veterinary practice in charge of over 30 employees. I spend all day taking care of other people, putting out fires, and wishing I could change my name for about twenty-four hours when I am in an office and hear "Mallary! We need you!" ringing down the hallways. When I get home from a sixteen hour day it is nice to have someone take care of me and to make no decisions whatsoever.

Whether you desire to be the breadwinner in a more equalitarian type of relationship or you have dreams of vacuuming in pearls and hosting bake sales these are all noble pursuits in the heart of a happy woman. Do not judge a woman who doesn't have the same aspirations as you. Be proud of her for knowing her own heart well enough to have aspirations.

Maybe you think you are the pack leader. I can speak to you with the knowledge of what I know from my leadership and administrative positions since my relationship pack leader status is limited. My mother once told me that it is important to remember in management that you console human error and punish negligence. I have told my employees the same thing as they weep over a mistake they made; a mistake that I want to wring their necks for but, instead, I give them a hug. To be in a position of power is to understand that you are only as good as the people supporting you. As a pack leader, you need your pack. Your instinct is probably to control every situation but you can't. Make sure you don't alienate the ones you have chosen to help you by thinking you are an island.

If you are going to be the leader, you must be worthy of being followed. You must never delegate more than you are in control of. You must be a leader and not a boss. It may be difficult to notice a difference in these words but it can be colossal. To put it in canine terms, if you are going to be pack leader that means that the person you are involved with is choosing to submit, and that decision should always be respected. Dogs will roll over and expose their belly to show submission. People tend to be subtler but you will see that they have made themselves vulnerable. They will allow you to lead. They will stop fighting over the parts of your togetherness that they are entrusting to you. This is a scary time in the establishment of your hierarchy while you wait to see if the person you are allowing to be in charge is going to become controlling and muster commands without explanation like a boss; or become a leader, in charge but also fighting the good fight along side of you. They give you reasons as to why the choices they made are the best for everyone, not just you and least of all themselves.

No one allows himself or herself to be ordered around for very long without a level of bitterness developing over time. You are with this person because you are in love with them, and although people think that all you need is love, it isn't. You need respect. A dog continually beaten and yelled at is apt to snap at someone eventually. There are times the person you share your bed with will not like you as much as they do today and they are capable of snapping. If that person respects you, they will give you more opportunities for you to make up for the times that you made them feel like following you was a mistake. You will need those opportunities to redeem yourself. You are human, and you will make mistakes. You will do wrongs to people that can be forgiven, but not forgotten. Admit your failures. Ask forgiveness. Be humble.

So much of the success of a relationship is wrapped up in this struggle of leader versus follower because the idea of submitting control to someone is terrifying no matter which side of that you are on. What if they fail you as pack leader? What if you fail them as a pack? Couples who dwell in these questions are often persistently at war. The pack leader is constantly being challenged because the pack does not want to submit and trust another's leadership, or the pack is defensive because they feel the leader has never proven that they are to be trusted. You can't be on both sides of the fence. Be the pack leader, and lead in a manner that provides for the ones around you or be the pack that invigorates your leader.

Pick a side. Then earn it.

Take Him To A Petsmar..... Random Corporate Pet Themed Store.

There is a corporate aspect to being an animal lover as well as a purely organic one. On the corporate side are our breeders, who may love animals, but are breeding and selling to make money. Most breeders, while attempting to have the best of intentions, can provide information that may not be the best from a medical standpoint. Like anyone in the veterinary profession, I have frequently had arguments with clients trying to undo the damage a misinformed breeder has done. A lot of this information is drawn from old wives tales. For instance, you can prevent heartworms or fleas by feeding your pet garlic. Just so you know, even small amounts of garlic will quickly throw your pet into an anemic episode that can be fatal. What about the old axiom that putting burnt oil on a dog will cure mange? I'm not entirely sure what burnt oil even is but I can guarantee you that it will not cure anything. All it will really do is make your dog greasy as fuck and smell like a dirty mechanic's shop.

While there are bad breeders, there are also good breeders. The good ones consider themselves not breeders, but pet owners and they are amazing owners at that. People who keep impeccable kennels that are clean enough to eat off of and harboring love in their hearts as they care about each and every single whelp they wean.

There is always another side to the mirror. There are less reputable breeders who flat out lie. They treat their animals strictly as assets, and it isn't just the animals that suffer. People who have paid inordinate amounts of money for sick or congenitally defective pets are now left with their feelings invested in a pet that may not live or might never be normal. If a breeder can't find homes for all the puppies in a litter, those are often sent off to a shelter when the new litter comes of age since they are now older and no longer likely to bring in a significant monetary amount.

At these shelters you will find the most organic of all animal lovers, our shelter volunteers. I think that shelters do an amazing job of finding homes for the unwanted animals of the world. I'm an absolute advocate of adoption over buying whatever the new designer dog of the week is. I used to work at a clinic that volunteered an affiliation with a local shelter. Our clinic did wellness exams for the newly adopted pets. Families would bring in their new puppy and their children would get to ask questions like why their new pet's nose is wet and how to get them to stop licking. We considered being able to inform these new owners about the ins and outs of pet ownership a great teaching opportunity.

As much of a fan of shelters as I am I believe that shelters can unintentionally set a pet and a family up for failure. Hear me out! Volunteers primarily staff shelters. Amazing volunteers take the time that they could be working paying hours at their regular job, spending with family and friends, taking care of a house or other hobbies, and devote that time to a cause that is a concern in every single city. Volunteers are saints. Volunteers are also trained on the fly and do the best they can. That being said, there are common misconceptions in veterinary medicine that one only learns with years of medical training and experience. Some examples of this are mistakenly assigning the age of pets based on size or attitude instead of on deciduous teeth loss or tarter levels, assigning breed based solely on coat or markings, instead of using this as only one factor, and predicting adult weight of a puppy based on these already wrong assumptions.

In working for this great company that allotted resources and time to help countless shelter pets, the staff would more than occasionally see a family bring in what was labeled as a nine pound puppy that was supposedly eight months old and close to full grown. In reality, a well-intentioned volunteer saw a black and brown small dog and knew these to be the markings of a miniature pincher, but didn't have the knowledge to check the teeth for age. If they had, they would have seen that this eight-month-old puppy still had a mouth full of baby teeth and was most likely a two-month-old shepherd mix puppy well on its way to being a seventy-five pound boss of a dog. These stories were countered by watching frat boy Alpha males bring in a newly adopted "Labrador" puppy with aspirations of duck hunting only to find out that newly named "Silverado" was actually a corgi mix, a breed with arguably the shortest legs on any breed of dog. Short legs make swimming out to retrieve ducks moderately more difficult. Not impossible, but not likely.

No volunteer looks at a puppy and said "I'm going to mislabel you so that your new family realizes you are the opposite of what they wanted after three children are already attached". Volunteers have an amount of love in their heart that is incomparable to paid employees in virtually any other profession. I have the upmost respect for these individuals. In fact, I bring up volunteers not to crucify their efforts but to segue into that, without any ill intentions, a family and a pet are set up for failure because they are basing compatibility on a very small amount of information and this information is often biased.

In this same way, despite the best of intentions, I think that modern day dating does nothing to help jumpstart a healthy relationship. All relationships start out the same way: with a meeting. This meeting can be online or in person, by browsing a pet finding website or seeing each other across a crowded a kennel or bar. You flirt, you pet, and then you go your separate ways. These first meetings are fun and inspiring and leave you with a sense of wonder and excitement about the future, but these meetings are only providing a small amount of information. They are an acknowledgement that you both like the same bar, that you both have pushy friends who drug you to a restaurant that you both hate, or you both happened to wear shirts supporting the same band. This small amount of information is a great place to start, but it needs to be just a starting point, and not the foundation of your future.

Society has accentuated us knowing very little about the person we are dating by glamourizing dates that teach us nothing about this person. Movies are great time fillers, but you are sitting in silence for upwards of two and a half hours and learn nothing except that he might have a great laugh or is at least gentlemen enough to give you the armrest. Even if you begin the evening with dinner before the movie there is often only about half an hour of true talk time between nervous banter about what you both are ordering, trips to the bathroom, and finding common ground in making fun of the waiter's vest. A group date is a great time but people inevitably fall into comfort zones with their separate groups of friends and end up with a slightly alienated view of the night. Of course your friends are fun, but you aren't here to get to know them. You already know them. You are supposed to be paying attention to

Mr. NewGuy, not spending the night trying to convince your best friend to not go home with his best friend. You have seen this play out before and know they will never want to see each other again after a one-night stand, which will therefore doom your new beau before he has had the chance to blossom.

Last on the list of standard dates is a bar. Please don't think I am speaking ill of what I consider to be my Mecca. A bar is a great time. It is potentially the best of times. Ever. My happiest moments have occurred in or because of bars, whether I remember them or not. The concern will be that looking at a night through beer goggles will make the whole thing seem more fun, more sexy, and will make you think that his mildly sexist jokes were much more hilarious than they actually were.

These will most likely be your first three dates, and you are doing yourself a massive disservice by tolerating this. Society teaches us this is ok! It sets us up for a major crash and burn when we don't fight against it. True first dates should be a foreshadowing of what is to come for the rest of your relationship. Whether it is by text or chat, call or sending carrier pigeons to set it up, you make plans. You find out if he is a guy that has interesting ideas of what a good date location is or if he wants you to plan it. A true first date is the two of you getting to know one another. This is a time for us to learn about each other's interests, hobbies, and families. You should be seeing if he pays more attention to his text messages than to you and if he pays for dinner. You should be having conversations and discovering that you have more in common than you liking to drink and he knowing which bar has specials that night of the week.

In the excitement that comes with starting to date someone, it is easy to get lost in the habit of these dinner-and-a-movie dates. Before you know it, you are at the third or fourth date. If you succumb to social norms, you are at the time where you are expected to make a physical decision but what do you really know about this person? Do you know enough to have sex with them? Do you know if you see a future with him yet? Obviously you like them enough to let him buy you drinks and maybe even spring for some yourself, but do you like him enough to add a number to your list? It's probably hard to say at this point, but I did figure out a way to thin the herd out a little bit.

I call it the Wal- the Petsma- The Random Generic Corporate Department Store Date. On the Random Generic Corporate Dep- Wow, avoiding trademark charges makes that the longest name like ever. Let's just call it the Mall Date. The point of the Mall Date is to force the presence of common interests and communication or to force the realization that you pretty much can't stand this person. Maybe can't stand is too harsh, but let's say you know you are not in love with the idea of this person anymore. If you can walk around a mall with someone completely sober, and make conversation that doesn't annoy either of you then you are a step ahead of most people who have already been dating for years. If you cannot only avoid being annoyed, but also stay entertained, you are light years into the future.

I would, by no means, be naïve enough to think that walking around a mall is going to lead to a walk down the aisle. This quest is not a cure all for your dating world. I have had plenty of my friends dismiss this little scheme of mine saying it weeds out a guy before I really know them. They say it is a waste of time or that I am too picky. The point of this is not to narrow down the man that you will one day marry. It is just meant to help clear out the ones who you definitely shouldn't. I spent a lot of my formative dating years wasting what I now know is very precious time because I was blind to the notion that I didn't like the man I was dating for upwards of ten dates or three months. I was what I like to call an alcohol enthusiast, better known as an alcoholic. Do you know who is fun, witty and entertaining when you are drunk? Everyone is. This can make it difficult to narrow down acceptable men to pursue and difficult to get rid of the ones less deserving of my attention in a timely manner.

The theory behind The Mall Date is simple enough. Find a time for him to go on a pointless shopping trip with you. Let's say you are in the vicinity of Mr. NewGuy. Maybe you have stayed the night and need an activity to kill time before lunch. "Let's hang out," you say. "What do you want to do?" he will inquire. "I don't know. I need to go to the mall. Want to come with me?" you will innocently respond as if this is not a critical part of expunging assholes from your life.

Arrive at the store or mall of your choosing. Pick from one or two items that you know to be cheap and on opposite sides of the store or in stores across the mall from each other. My go-to items were Starbucks and shoes. Pro tip, if you want to save some money in the long run, tell your Mall Date that the shoes don't fit and you are going to wait to buy them. Otherwise, you end up with a new pair of shoes every month.... Or I guess an even more Pro-pro-tip is to just buy the shoes!

Take Mr. NewGuy to the department stores or sections of your choice, and make no less that two trips around. Do not attempt this when you are in a hurry. If you have dinner reservations or need to be at the theater at a certain time, this is an endeavor best avoided. It will start a fight if he feels like you guys need to rush and you are trying to leisurely lead him around with no clear plan. I used to give myself an hour to walk around before we needed to leave to be anywhere. An hour means plenty of time to drink a coffee and try on a pair of anything. It is plenty of time to go into a store he might want to visit. It will give you time to see how he treats the store clerks or how he responds when there is a family walking slower than hamsters in peanut butter in front of you. I have learned so much about the people I was dating with this little game. I learned quickly which guys were only hanging out with me for the fun parts. They wanted to rush me around and leave as quickly as possible so they could whisk us away to a bar or to hang out with other friends. There was no room for leisure for them in this experiment, and it became evident that they only wanted me in an intoxicated setting. There is no hope for a future in that.

I learned which ones were narcissistic or cruel in the way they dealt with the people around them, or in the way they shopped. There is always some fun in people watching and making little comments about those around you. "That person has a funny shirt on. That person thinks they are so cool with their mismatched hipster clothes. Oh goodness, those children, do you remember when we were in high school and thought we were that cool?" This is all normal social commentary. But there were some men who picked only weak targets, such as a person who had an obvious handicap, or someone who became the subject of cruel words because of their appearance. Maybe they were overweight or wearing something that garnered jokes about religious background. I am quick to make an inappropriate joke about a cougar in Victoria's Secret and I will stand behind thinking and expressing that the salesman in the shoe store had hair like *The Weekend*. However, I have been in the presence of men who made people watching a window into their own timid masculinity. It didn't make me laugh or think they were impressive as a man. It only opened my eyes to how they acted like this in all situations, not just to impress me or to seem confident; it only personified insecurities. At that point, no amount of alcohol was going to hide that they would make the same offensive joke about the bartender later that evening and that all of their frat guy friends would laugh.

Seemingly most important, I learned which ones were dull, just plain dull. I have always thrived on witty dialogue. I've always loved when there is unforced ebb and flow to a conversation. One topic eases into the next easily and allows for this give and take. Some guys don't have that. Some people don't need it. Some women are happy to have lulls in conversation as a way to collect their thoughts or so they have plenty of time to prepare their next line of speech. I have always hated that! I've always hated quiet. Even now as I am alone in a house typing on a keyboard, I have a window playing random episodes of early 2000s sitcoms behind my document, and although I am not watching it or really even listening to it, my mind will screech to a halt when it stops auto-playing and I am left with the hollow sound of silence. I wanted a man that found it possible to have an entire conversation about nothing; someone that can fill an afternoon with witty banter that may not have any merit other than keeping us both entertained. If a guy can't feed off the high energy at a mall and make meaningless conversation while people watching, then he will never be able to keep me occupied while sitting on a couch and performing our own version of Mystery Science

Theater 3000 to B-grade horror movies on Netflix. Knowing that early on helps set my relationship up for success.

It's important to start your relationship out on the right foot. Find ways to connect on levels that are deeper than big ass beer night. Find conversations that lead to experiences. Find experiences that lead to memories. And in that, you'll find someone that you want to be around for longer than your buzz lasts.

Potty Pads Just Teach Him To Shit In The House.

Potty pads are an interesting invention. A potty pad is a two foot by two foot plastic lined, fibrous pad laced with pheromones to attract your fluffy FiFi and train her to know the correct spots to go ... potty. This sounds brilliant. Your pet is drawn to use the bathroom on these and not your shag rug. While I am not a fan of this product, it does serve a great function in the veterinary community as a fantastic liner for the cages and kennels of our less hygienic patients. Potty pads make it easy for us to promise you that your pet is always in a sanitary environment without driving the overnight technician crazy as they try so hard to keep your sick pet's kennel clean.

At home, they are intended to be a training tool used when you absolutely cannot venture outside with your pet, but how often do our intentions go as planned? What ends up happening is that you pay twenty dollars a week to let your pet defile your house. Potty pads are marketed to regular people as a training tool but are more often purchased by the busy professional who cannot be bothered to take a new puppy outside and wait while it sniffs all the leaves in the yard until it finds the perfect one to urinate on. These CEOs, instead, find it agreeable to train their dog exactly where inside the house they would like it relieve itself. Essentially, you are training your pet to use the bathroom on your floor. Awesome side note is that puppies love to shred them. Imagine coming home to urine and feces soaked strips of plastic and cotton covering kennels or kitchen floors. Are you excited about them yet?

Another great side effect happened to a client of mine. Mrs. YogaMom came in to the clinic one day and requested the name of our clinic behaviorist. Knowing she had a nine-month-old, well-behaved, very designer dog I inquired as to what the problem was. Apparently, little Billy YogaMom has been putting together a project about the founding fathers. This project involves large sheets of poster board, and little FiFi had taken to treating these sheets of poster board in the same manner that she treats her potty pad as a toilet.

Can you blame little FiFi? When you have to go, you have to go. When you are trained to go on square shaped pads on the floor you seldom stop determine if this particular square shaped pad has absorbent cotton underlay or if it is a synopsis of Thomas Jefferson's Louisiana Purchase. This is what FiFi has been trained to do. This is the reason we humans prefer to go potty in a clean bathroom and not at a truck stop. It's what we are trained to do.

In *Sit Means Sit*, we discussed a friend of mine that made a habit of changing her entire personality after dating anyone for six months, effectively ruining what she had built with her man. She was training her man in a specific way early in their courtship. She was training him to believe that he was the center of her universe. So can you blame the guy when he wants to act like it? Just like we can train FiFi to do things that we end up hating, we can create a bad behavior in a person. So, what are you training your significant other to do?

We all want to hate the man who is currently leaving our friend home to watch the baby alone all the time while he goes off with his friends. We hate that we lost girl's night, and we hate that she cries when we have it. We hate that we don't have our best friend to tell us that yes, our ass does look terrible in the skinniest jeans ever sewn together *before* we leave the dressing room and run into the hot assistant manager. We hate that they are not there to inform us that no, we cannot pull off faux fur. But it is unfair to train a person that an action is acceptable and then punish them for it. Let's go back a little in their time together.

When they were dating, she never made him act like a couple. He went on impulsive trips with his friends without informing or inviting her. He made it a habit to frequent bars and concerts alone leaving her at home until he arrived at her place more than tipsy at three in the morning. It is normal for a twenty something year old male to want to live his own life. Both you and he should be able to trust each other in time apart. But is it okay every weekend? It must have been, because she said nothing.

So then he proposes, and she says yes, and now they are engaged. They move in together and while she is keeping the house immaculately clean, he still goes out with his friends. He plays basketball all weekend and enjoys a cold one with the boys before coming home late to a lukewarm dinner she wanted to serve an hour ago. He is obviously committed since he proposed, but when does this schedule leave time for the two of them as a couple? It doesn't, but that's okay because she says nothing.

Now they are married and have a baby. While he still wants to go out with his friends and get drunk at the beach, she finally decides that she needs him to be her partner and a father. She now finally decides to say something.

As anyone would have guessed, this new set of rules will be met with resistance, heavy resistance: offended, fear-induced, angry resistance from both parties.

These actions do need to change, and they need to change on both ends, not just his. You are not blameless for allowing the behavior for so long. You obviously can't continue to be miserable, but you have to understand why change will be difficult. It will not just be recognizing a fault in the relationship and fixing it. Once it becomes a mutual habit, you are going to have to become different people from the ones that created the situation. It will include retraining yourself and your partner to change the dynamics of your household. It will take both of you actively reconstructing the way you see each other and *no one* likes to change.

So how do you do this?

We start this process with a *lot* of talking. Not just flapping your jaw at him, but a constructive expression of feelings that will penetrate and engage. As women we walk a fine line between nagging and communicating. We walk that line deciding whether or not to yell because he didn't wash the spinach and put it away like we asked, and now it's wilted and gross. We try to pick our battles, but it can be hard for us to see what side of that line we are on when we are upset and need to talk. Facilitating the right kind of communication is both the key and the challenge.

In a perfect world, both people would actively seek change together. What is more common, however, is one person must decide to independently change their lifestyle despite the fact that the other is not going to. Without careful consideration, you can end up continually nagging and he will end up continually defensive. Just like we train bad behavior in others, we can train good behavior in ourselves. Start there.

Train yourself to use better words. Instead of making accusations about problems or complaining about the lack of communication, speak engaging words and ask simple questions. “I’d love for you to tell me about your day” sounds so much nicer than “We never talk when you get home”. “How was work?” is going to be met with “fine” which does not facilitate further topics. If you ask questions that require more than a yes or no answer you will learn more about his day, leading to more in depth questions over the next few days. These are called open-ended questions. Don’t try to have an hour of conversation in the first day. Ask one or two open-ended questions and then say “Thank you for telling me that. I love hearing about your day.” Positive encouragement is important.

Train yourself to have a beneficial attitude while saying the words you choose. It is completely okay to be upset when something is said that you find annoying or frustrating, but remember that you get back what you give. If when starting off you do not get the response you want, and then you get snippy, you will be met with a return of snippy tones. If it means that you have to stay silent for fifteen seconds between each line you speak, it will be worth the extra time it takes to calm your voice and plan your response. Those extra fifteen seconds might add an extra thirty minutes to the dialog but more productive conversation is worth the extra time the conversation will take.

Train yourself to leave a conversation in a way that does not hinder the resolution. When you notice a talk is progressing into an argument that is getting out of hand, recognize that you both need to take break. Take a breath. Say the words "I feel like I need to step away for a minute but I love you, and I do want to work this out. Can I come back in five minutes?" After this statement, leave enough time for him to answer yes, or start to pout and then walk out of the room. You need to be able to collect your thoughts and be able to come back to this subject with a clear head. When either of you becomes too emotional the listening stops. Even if you are right, if either of you stop listening you can't work anything out. Calm yourself down enough that you can listen to what he is saying, and hopefully in that time he will do the same. Then, go back to the conversation. This is the important part. Do not run away and leave problems as problems. Do not yell and scream and accuse. Work toward a solution to your problem instead of rehashing whose fault it was to begin with. Think forward, not backward. It doesn't matter who started this quarrel. It matters that you finish it together. You can train each other to speak with respect by speaking with respect to each other.

And finally, train yourself to focus on what you can do and what you can't. You are the only one you have any control over. You can set a good example. You can influence someone else's behavior by approaching situations with a calm, practical nature. You can show people how you want to be treated by how you treat them, but in the midst of all of these things that you can do, you will not change someone without their consent. You cannot force them to be reasonable or get them to put in the effort you think they are missing. You cannot continue to be responsible for the entirety of the problems or solutions in this relationship. You must accept that you can only change yourself and hope this someone you love so much changes with you. If they don't, you are going to need to start thinking about removing yourself from this circumstance if it continues to deteriorate.

I don't want people to read this chapter and think that I am endorsing becoming a doormat to be walked all over and yelled at while you wait around patiently like a 1950s housewife to see if he is going to change. At the same time, I don't want you to believe that I want you to attempt to change your partner for a week and then when the results aren't immediate that I give you permission to leave him. I want you to take inventory of the pros, cons, and possibilities of where you are right now in this moment. I want you to be honest with your mate about how happy you actually are right now. Be honest with your mate about how long you can stay at this level of happiness. Then, be honest with yourself about these things as well. Know that whatever level of happiness you both are at, it can get better. I want you to know that there is hope for almost any couple in my opinion, barring abuse. Your solution may take longer or take a different route than someone else's but as long as both people want to grow together then you can.

One of my worst and best relationships was with a man that taught me how to work through an argument and come out stronger on the other end. He might have been a lying bastard but that lying bastard is the reason that I communicate with my husband so well, and I swear I owe that man a debt of gratitude. Without him making me tell him all the reasons I was mad and didn't want to talk to him, I wouldn't currently be able to express my feelings and avoid a screaming match. This man gave me time to collect my thoughts but refused to let me sweep anything under the rug and avoid talking about it, which is exactly what Past Mallary was best at. He trained me to be a better mate. I wouldn't be able to tell my husband, without coming off as a bitch, that I think all the broken electronics he keeps in his office are stupid. On a serious note, honey, I know you will never fix them, you know you will never fix them, and they need to be thrown away.

You need to refine your fight style. An ounce of prevention is worth a pound of cure. Hone your prevention. Knowing how to fight constructively will lengthen the time that you go between fights. You will find yourself starting to apply these prevention tactics to matters before fights begin. You will inject this thought process into the way you speak to each other everyday and you will be astounded at the results.

The only downfall to having an excellent argument style is it will massively kill your make up sex game. I happen to think connected, passionate sex the rest of the year is worth missing out on that "we almost lost each other" make-up sex. As good as that clutching emotional fuck is at night, it comes at the cost of knowing that you are not working on making things better during the day. Make up sex is simply giving yourself a reward for what you just went through. I would gladly miss out on a few good lays to know I would be sleeping next to this man for the rest of my life instead of spending my nights wishing I could roll over and touch him but knowing that we are slowly beginning to hate each other.

Guys Love Bitches. We all do.

At emergency veterinary hospitals across the nation, there is at least one dog every night that comes in that needs a "party hat". In veterinary lingo, a party hat is a muzzle. Party hat tends to sound more playful and clients prefer a cutesy euphemism over hearing technicians say we are going to shove this circular vinyl fabric around your pet's mouth, holding its jaws together so that we are not ripped limb from limb by your aggressive four pound Pomeranian mix. To be clear, by Pomeranian mix I mean a hideous combination of four breeds, one of which is the Pomeranian, that someone paid too much money for from Craigslist.

It is a similar dog each night. Usually, it is an undersized breed that has never been made to walk on a leash; held the majority of the time so its pristine paws have rarely touched ground. This bitch hates everyone but her owner. You can almost see the lasers shooting out of its eyes as soon as you walk into the room. This dog embodies the phrase "if looks could kill". Despite this, the owner still tries to hand you the dog, swearing that Killer is the sweetest pet she has ever owned and that she has never torn the flesh off the hands or faces of any innocent bystanders.

You know better.

You know that as soon as you reach to help this dog you will be down a digit on your right hand. And yet, the owner is blinded to this, even as they witness the lunge from their shoulder to your jugular. They swear she is just shy, that she feels threatened, that she feels protective of her owner and just wants mommy all to herself. They pile on the excuses in defense of their precious Killer.

No matter how many pre-meditated reasons for this behavior they will attempt to persuade you with, you are very aware that the pet most likely acts like this any time it is in a veterinary practice. It also probably acts like this whenever the owners have company at the house, and also when Mrs. Owner's downtrodden husband attempts to get anywhere near his wife. You will never convince this owner that Killer is dangerous or that she needs to instill limitations on this kind of behavior. As soon as the owner tries to do this, Killer will flash those puppy dog eyes, shyly snuggle in close, and roll over on her back. The owner will forgive and forget. You will be faced with the same conversation at the next meeting, which you pray will not be for a very long time.

Now read through that again and make a few mental changes. Firstly input "new girlfriend" anywhere I wrote dog, Killer, or bitch. Actually, well, you can probably leave bitch. It's appropriate for both circumstances. Secondly input, "platonic guy friend" or "hopefully future husband" into the owner's role in this narrative.

We've all been there. You see this situation present itself in a couple of different ways. You see it when you begin dating a guy who is still hung up on his terrible human being of an ex. If his insecurities allow it to progress past the first few dates, you get to act as counselor for the first six months you date him. You may also notice this when your platonic male friend starts dating a new girl, and she's terrible. Even if you could get past new girl completely altering the personality of your platonic male friend, you recognize that he is mostly miserable with her. None of your altruistic attitude matters anyways because new girl hates you. She hates you in a seething, unbalanced way that she will express in unrelenting passive aggression. Maybe you offended her in some way, and maybe you didn't. You may never know the origin. What you do know is that this girl is a bitch.

I hate to break it to you, but she will probably always be a bitch, and he will love her despite her being a bitch until he doesn't anymore. Unfortunately, that's the best time frame I can give you. Until he realizes the bitch-ness of it all, you will be forced to smile at her and pretend to get along for his sake. You both will.

What makes an owner love a dog that is dangerous? What makes a man love a bitch?

We think that if we knew the answers to the "why's" it would make us feel better. Why do our friends allow this? Why do these friends that we love allow themselves to be taken advantage of by bitchy mates and treated in a way that we deem unfit? Why do our friends accept weakness and instead of persevering as the strong role model we accept advice from? We fight so hard on our friends' behalf against seeing them accept this kind of exhausting treatment that when they acquiesce to it, we often push them away in name of trying to protect them. What we are really trying to protect is our image of them. Now, before you go getting' all high and mighty, I can give you my gold star guarantee that your friends have had these same musings about some troglodyte that you were dating. Some person who you were dating brought out the worst in you and made you weak with love. Instead of wondering only about your friends, you need to include yourself in these musings. You need to be asking yourself how *we* make these errors in judgment. How do *we* allow ourselves to be treated like this? Why do *we* accept weakness instead of strength?

Instead of focusing on this friend who is dating Cujo, allow me to switch pronouns for a few paragraphs and focus on the group. Let us understand why we all let ourselves act this way. In doing so, we can feel a little better about our friends acting this way. I have seen myself and my friends complete this cycle many times, and I have read a number of articles- well, titles of articles that explain this phenomenon. There is a theory that subconsciously we will put ourselves in the same circumstances over and over again so that we give ourselves the opportunity to change the tide and fight for a different outcome. The idea is that the subjects of your most terrible relationships mirror either a maternal or paternal figure from your childhood and the issues you had with them. Your subconscious knows that in order to break this cycle of unhealthy relationships, you must defeat the demons from your past. If you had an overbearing mother, you might continually choose a domineering mate and need to stand up to them. If you had an abusive father, you may choose a cruel partner so you can understand you are not to blame and that you are strong enough to leave.

Each time we choose a bad breed of man we wonder why. Why did I not recognize the same traits in this man that broke my heart last time? It's like childbirth. You only remember the joy of holding that baby in your arms, and you immediately forget that you were physically pained to the equivalent of breaking bone. This compulsion to relive a nightmare may be why we pick the same kind of breed every time. Your brain knows you need to once again walk through the fire of these historical conditions in order to spark the realization you shouldn't be burned any more. The only problem with your brain is that it might not realize you aren't ready yet to take action before you get hurt.

You might still be young and you have not been through enough relationships to realize you have a destructive pattern that needs to be addressed. You might not be aware of specific negative issues or you are avoiding them. You might be so self-involved that you don't see that the problem is you, but just like Taylor Swift, when there is a long list of failed relationships there has to be a common thread fueling these breakups. That thread is you. You need to acknowledge your own demons to be able to fight them. You need to expect the attack in order to fight to the best of your ability. Until you are ready to recognize your faults and attraction to poor partners, you will continue to put yourself through a series of degrading, powerless relationships.

Unfortunately, youth is not an excuse. This experience has no time limit. We like to think we grow out of choosing poor suitors simply by aging but until you narrow down the problem and learn the pros and cons of your choices you are doomed to repeat them. I love to make the haughty statement when gossiping about a person's particular predicament that "I made that same mistake… when I was twenty," and then I scoff, snort, and snicker like I'm so much better than these poor, single people. I'm not. It's arrogant to think like that. That myself, or anyone in a happy marriage, pretends that we don't have issues that could easily disgrace our marriages if made public is ridiculous. We are capable of making others and ourselves miserable, often without any realization of doing so. We are all human, and we are no better than those that we surround ourselves with. If you are surrounding yourself with assholes, dig deep and find out why. The "why" might be closer than you'd like.

You might find it comforting to know that your brain believes in you, even if your heart doesn't know what it is looking for yet. While your heart is busy making the same mistakes over and over again, your brain knows it is smart enough to steer you in the right direction as long as the rest of you can ignore your heart. Your brain believes in you so fervently that it always is certain "this time is the one. That pesky heart will figure it out with this one and we'll never have to go through this again." Your cerebrum knows that the only way to work out your past mistakes is by facing them head on. You need to be in the moment and fight your way through it; confronting all the problems you were never able to face in your youth.

Remember, after reading *Sit Means Sit,* that making an all-powerful list of the things you require of a man or a relationship can help you isolate the characteristics you might be wishing to seek. The list is only part one. Part two is recognizing these items from your list in a good man and ignoring the strikingly handsome loser that happens to possess one or two admirable qualities. So often we think that a nice guy can't contain all the traits that turn us on, that a guy who respects us can't make our toes curl in bed or a man that is financially sound has to be boring. This is entirely false, but when you receive the response you want, the response is all you see. We become almost superstitious in our beliefs that a certain type of man is unable to possess certain qualities. We think that a man who responds when we are upset is a man who cares; instead we should see that we shouldn't have had to get upset in order for him to pay attention to us. We think that a man who can make us laugh when we are mad is a man who wants to make us happy. In reality, we should recognize that a man who wanted us happy would have worked to not make us mad.

Your platonic male friend who has begun dating this new girl may only see a beautiful woman who lets him watch football, cleans his apartment, and impresses his co-workers with cookies. He might have trouble right now seeing the raging mommy issues he is harboring by dating a rampant bitch who does his laundry after two weeks of dating. As I've mentioned before, in a case where it comes down to you or the bitch, you are going to end up in the doghouse. Bide your time. In a future chapter, *When Is It Time To Euthanize?,* we will get you some better instructions on how to speak your peace in a way that will alleviate the burden of truth you are keeping in, with the goal of keeping you in good graces with your dear friend. At this point in time it is uncouth to put a muzzle on a human without their written and verbal consent. The best thing you can do is to let your friend know how you feel in a private, civilized manner, reassure them you will slap a smile on your face whenever Cujo is around, and take a lot of deep breaths.

Also, side note, you may be at least a little in love with your "platonic" guy friend. See further research to dispute this in the forms of: Adele's first two albums; the movies *Some Kind of Wonderful*, *Win a Date With Tad Hamilton*, or *Made of Honor*; read *Emma* by Jane Austen and watch *Emma* with Gweyth Paltrow.

If You Give A Dog A Cookie....

This is going to be a fun chapter. It is all about sex. I am going to use small words for this first part because as soon as I said "sex" you started thinking about your last really good lay and lost your ability to comprehend detailed thought. Sex is fun. Very fun. Even sex that cannot be classified as mind-blowing is still pretty fun. It is so much fun that we get stupid. Very stupid. We get so stupid that we make bad decisions and think they are good ones, when they are not. Okay, I'll return back to using normal words.

In order to combat some of these bad decisions, I want to imagine the little words from the Bud Light billboard requesting that you "Enjoy responsibly" whenever you start to get excited about sex. This chapter is going to focus on using sex as a bargaining chip and why that is terrible and also really effective. I want you to understand why using sex as a weapon and using sex as a Band-Aid to cover up the issues you are ignoring are both wrong.

Just like our last chapter, this all comes down to you training each other to know what is important. When you get a new puppy, you and the puppy will instantly start training each other. Your pup will learn to potty outside and to sit before you feed him. You will learn that when you stop petting his belly before he is ready, your hand will be met with adorable head-butts because he wasn't finished getting love. You will both teach the other what you like and what you don't. You will reward these good behaviors, as he gets better at them. He will learn which activities are not rewarded and will begin to avoid them. Positive reinforcement tends to work better than negative. For pets this typically means food and praise. For men, it means boobs. It always means boobs.

Chewing up inappropriate items in the house tends to be the earliest presenting and most destructive problems with our new puppies. We buy them the most expensive "indestructible" Kong toys and a variety of bones in the shapes of dinosaurs and big rig tires, and yet they still only want to shred the expensive power cords used for our phones, laptops, and televisions, or the irreplaceable feet of our couches and antique arm chairs. I have seen dogs chew holes in sheet rock clear to the next room or destroy the frame of a door in mere minutes.

There is a frequent error when training a chewing puppy. Our instinct is to take away the object the puppy shouldn't be gnawing on and replace it with something on which they are actually supposed to be chomping. We like to take away our new patent leather stilettos and replace them with a rawhide or other suitable chew toy. In doing this, we are punishing our pups by giving them a tasty treat. That makes no sense. Think about it. When they go potty outside, we give them a snausage. When they sit, stay, and rollover we give them a rawhide. When they chew on something we don't want them to destroy we reward them with something delicious? That's terrible training. Your pet will be thoroughly confused. He will have no idea he did anything wrong for so long that by the time you get fed up and exasperated, he is still trying to figure out what his mistake was in the first place. It's like punishing me with caramel turtle cheesecake when I don't go to the gym.

If you give a dog a cookie, he will think he did something right. We have to eliminate the use of a cookie when it is not proper. We shouldn't use the absence of sex as a punishment when we don't get our way. We also shouldn't use the presence of sex as a Band-Aid to hide that we are upset and are only petting that puppy so it doesn't run away. When we get to the place where our dispute has fizzled into uneasy tension, and we are not pleased but are no longer yelling, the rest of our evening can be hard to navigate. As a woman, we don't want to be the reason we have started bellowing at each other for the second time in one night, but we can't deny that things are obviously not normal and are not resolved. We need to lean into that abnormal evening instead of trying to act like everything is fine. Other than you knowing it will make the dog happy, what good does it do you to placate him with a treat when you are pissed off at his earlier actions? I think withholding sex to get what you want is completely counter productive to fruitful interaction however I think that fucking him when you are angry and don't even really like him very much is a form of lying, if only to yourself. No, actually, mostly to him. If he comes home to a house that is spotless, a dinner that is warm on the table, and a wife who is dynamite in the sack, how is he supposed to know that you are still pissed about the fight you didn't finish? Stop setting him up for failure by letting him think everything is fine. If you continually mollify the household and he never knows there is a problem, when you finally overflow with rage from years of unresolved issues, he will be blindsided and you will only have yourself to blame for his ignorance of how you have felt this entire time.

We want our pups to know what they can do to make us happy, because when we are happy, they are happy, even if they don't realize it yet. Both people's joy is important but more than you as individuals; the happiness of you together is what is crucial. In the long run, neither of you will be happy if the root of a problem is not resolved. So resolve it.

This is where a lot of women think I am telling you to not have sex with him until he tells you that you won the fight and you get what you want; I am telling you to fix the problem instead of fucking around it. The difference in not fucking him when you are mad and using sex as a weapon is a precarious ledge. The specific difference is whether or not you are planning on bringing up the fight again and mutually work towards a solution. This doesn't mean you are forbidden to have sex until the fight is over or that you can't take a break and get some sleep, but always have an end game where you have come to a conclusion in the controversy.

There are times that I've wanted, nay, needed to just get some sleep after a particularly stressful bout of arguing, even if it is not over. I've needed to sit in my quiet mind and mull over everything that happened, but know this: There is a reason that "Never let the sun set on your anger" or "don't go to bed mad" are age-old pieces of advice that get written into every guest book at every wedding by more than a handful of people. When something exists for a long time it is because there is something of substance to back it up. They say this because they know that as soon as you go to bed, either to sleep or surrender to carnal desires, it is very likely that the fight will never reach a place of conclusion and will be swept under a rug to rot. If you go to bed angry and then wake up accepting the silence and small talk over breakfast, whatever caused this squabble will keep reoccurring. You have not fixed the problem, and you are establishing a precedent in which he is able to stall conclusions or decisions until he can coerce you into the sheets. If at any point "let's sleep on it because things will look better in the morning" becomes a habit and you then allow the argument to be swept under the rug by the light of the next day, you have fashioned a model that he will strive to replicate at every turn. The disappointment will continue.

When you are lying in your marital bed, mentally exhausted from the disappointment and emotion of a big fight, it is not absurd to think that either of you wouldn't want to roll over and fall into the arms of the person you love so dearly. There are plenty of reasons you would still have sex with him when you are fighting. You might really want to have sex. You recognize that you might need a break from the conflict, and you feel a strong desire to feel connected to him, even if you are upset. You might be ovulating and despite the fight you two are having there is still a plan to have a baby. You might really just want to have sex! There is nothing wrong with longing for the clear head, absent of thought, that sex brings and giving in to the rush of endorphins and relaxation that follows. If this is the case, then know that you both should be still planning on actively seeking a resolution to whatever this fight is as soon as possible, preferably within the next twenty-four hours. Twenty-four hours is well within the realms of saying, "We never came to a conclusion yesterday and I'd love to discuss it more now that we have had some time to cool down".

You can see how sex too soon after a quarrel can be a bad idea. You are putting a Band-Aid on a stab wound. Hopefully, you are not actively participating in dodging the discord between the two of you. If you feel confident that you are fixing your problems as they arise, the next step in healthy sex is to ensure that you are not using sex as a weapon.

You will know if you are using sex as a weapon if the verdict is going to be unilaterally beneficial and easy to misinterpret as a form of payment. It is something that primarily you will benefit from and can often be material in nature. When he doesn't do the dishes like you asked, or he tells you that you can't spend a thousand dollars on a Gucci fanny-pack, and you vow that his penis will remain untouched until you get an empty sink or the fanny-pack in tan with brown accents, these would be examples of using sex as a weapon. *Note*: Couture fanny-packs are an actual thing, except they are called belt bags, and they really are that expensive.

If you only have sex with him to reward him for a specific task and not because you genuinely love him, you are using sex as currency. Using sex as a form of currency is using sex as a weapon. Using sex as a weapon will only weaken the pillars of your foundation. Despite the premise of this entire book, men are not dogs. If you only give a man a little treat when you get something out of it, you are creating a situation where he is purchasing your body. You are his friend, his girlfriend, his fiancé, his wife, and his fuck buddy even, but you are not his prostitute. If you only want to fuck him when he performs a chore or he gives you a present maybe you don't actually want to fuck him.

Sex is always fun, but healthy sex is better. Don't base your intimacy on the currency of sex. Don't use this beautiful act meant to bring you close to your partner as the thing that covers up all of your problems and eventually drives you apart. Give that puppy a treat, but only when you know you will both be excited about it.

Admit Your Pet Is Sick. Take it to the doctor.

I've never worked in human medicine, but if it is anything like the veterinary field then no one ever goes to the doctor. We are convinced we know better than what any "doctor" will tell us about how sick we may or may not be. Veterinarians and veterinary technicians will open a new thermometer to take their own temperature, or in the most desperate of instances, will wrap a used one in cling wrap more than a few times. We will ask one of the vets on duty to listen to our lungs to make sure there are no crackles or wheezes and tell us haven't come down with pneumonia. Then, if you check the medical records on these particular employees' pets, it seems that suddenly their largest dog has an upper respiratory infection and needs antibiotics. We scrub our scratches and bite wounds with surgical cleanser, and then wrap our arms in bandage and cast material. We go so far as to hook ourselves up to fluids after a hangover and drink barium when we have heartburn. We are a very resourceful bunch. We are the same resourceful bunch that reminds you when you call us with a vomiting dog that you need to see the veterinarian, an actual doctor. We recommend that you take your beloved pet to someone who has gone through specialized schooling and has years of experience in treating sick pets and prescribing medications based on a physical exam. On some level we understand the hypocrisy of this situation, but we seldom want to think about it.

When working at an emergency clinic we are forced to avoid this hypocrisy every day. People call and due to limited funds or proximity to the clinic they inform you that they absolutely cannot under any circumstances come in to see the vet. They want the technician to give them medical advice over the phone or let them know how they can begin treatment at home. They beg for us to tell them doggie doses for over the counter human medications or tell them that the pain medications they have leftover from a skiing injury three years ago are safe for their dog. What they really want is for us to say is, "Yes, it can wait until morning to see your regular vet" and "No, you don't need to come in at three am". We simply can't do it.

As much as we want to reassure you that your pet is fine and that yes, most of those human pain medications are the exact same that we prescribe in the clinic, we can't. Apart from being illegal to diagnose an illness, or prescribe or advise medication without doing an exam, there are so many maladies that present as regular everyday occurrences. A snakebite, which can be fatal, will swell the same way as a bee sting, which is annoying but rarely causes death. A dog that meanders into your living room while you are binge watching *Game of Thrones* belching and acting oddly with a swollen belly could have gotten into a bag of treats and eaten five times the serving size, or your dog's stomach could have flipped into a gastric torsion and they could have less than a few hours to live without critical abdominal surgery. As much as we would love to give you specific advice without seeing your dog in the flesh, we can't do you the injustice of potentially giving you really bad advice following really good intentions. All we are able to do is recommend these owners take their pet to see a veterinarian as soon as they can so their pet can get some help. And, no, you can't send us a picture.

One of the hardest parts about being a pet owner and deciding to bring your pet into the clinic is admitting your pet has a problem. Just like the first step of admitting you are an addict is recognizing that you need a professional, the best thing you can do to help your pet is recognize that your pet needs help. Owners don't wait too long on purpose. Many of the very ill pets we see are presented with the same response from the owners: "We just thought she'd get better on her own." It's not that they didn't care or that they weren't attentive to the presence of a problem or that they didn't have the money. It's that they didn't recognize that the problem was not getting any better. They assumed everything would get worse for a bit and then resolve on its own, and it rarely does. This same owner may have called us multiple times asking about symptoms, and we most likely gave them the grand original advice to bring their pet in to see a doctor since it was getting worse. At this point, the owner retorts "well, it isn't worse, it's just not better," and every tech in the clinic collectively shakes their head in frustration. We know that five minutes before closing the clinic on Friday evening this owner is going to call and emphatically insist that it can't wait any longer. They will then need to rush in for this sudden emergency.

It is always easier to give advice than to take it. Just like we, as members of the veterinary field, refuse to see a doctor but find it easy to tell you to take your pet to a vet, it can be easy to tell a friend that they should see a marriage counselor while ignoring all the faults in your relationship.

The bible has a verse in Matthew that questions why you would point out the speck of sawdust in your brother's eye but ignore the plank protruding out of your own. It's a comical description when you think too much about it, but we do this every day. We do this when we visit a friend's house and silently judge the sink full of dirty dishes, knowing full well that we are soon to develop a serious gnat problem in our own kitchen on account of all the fruit bits left in three days worth of dirty glasses from your new fad smoothie diet. We do this when we joke about our friend's overweight dog while ours has been off of heartworm preventative for a year. We do this when we tell our friend that the continuous fights her husband and she have are more than enough reason for them to see a therapist, yet we ignore that our own house is chock full of passive aggressive quips and deafening silence.

It is so much easier to give advice than to listen and apply it to our own lives. That we may have failed in a matter as important as the rest of our lives is a terrifying insight, and we hate to admit it. We often refuse to see it until it is too late. People, even friends, often do each other a disservice by never mentioning that perhaps therapy would benefit you because the stigma of fear so heavily engrained in the words. I've heard multitudes of people, male and female, recoil as if bitten at the prospect of therapy and refuse to believe that counseling leads to anything but flat out, straight divorce. And in fact, these rumors are not entirely wrong. Statistics come in vastly different ranges, but I have heard stated that more than thirty-five percent of couples who attend couples counseling will get divorced within four years. That seems to be an astonishing number! You should let me break that down before you begin texting your friend and spouting off how you "knew" that counseling was a terrible idea and this Mallary girl thinks so, too! Well, slow your roll. You are wrong and therapy is awesome.

If you are a person who refuses to even consider therapy, you exude a palpable dread that someone might suggest counseling to you. I guarantee your friends pick up on that. I understand this dread. I felt it before my husband and I attended our first therapy session. It is a terrifying notion that someone with a degree and letters after their name might tell you, not just that you made a mistake, but that you should leave this mistake in your past and not look back, when every fiber of your being is telling you to hold tight to this "mistake" that you love so much and protect it. When our only response is to be defensive, we resist not just help from a trained counselor but from anyone. Like a dog that needs lifesaving medication will clamp down on all four hundred and fifty pounds per square inch of force in their jaw to prevent us from helping to save its life, we will resist what could potentially save our marriage. We will withdraw from our friends and family, pretending that our relationship doesn't need attention because it isn't getting worse and deny ourselves how much better it could be. Instead, we wait until the breaking point, and what could be the final hours of our relationship, when we can no longer contain how much worse things have gotten. Then we call in a professional and want them to fix us right away because now it's an emergency. Why are we surprised when someone, even someone with a degree and letters behind their name, cannot remold what we have warped in secret?

We wait too long. We drag ourselves under the shed and hide from the world. By the time we recognize the need for a mediator we have allowed our communication and our love for one another to deteriorate so badly that there may be too much resentment and hurt to recover. In many instances, by the time you both accept that you need help and have needed it a long time ago, there is a good chance that one of you has already mentally or emotionally given up. Once one of you has given up you won't even have a foundation to rebuild on. For this reason therapy seems to fail much more often than it succeeds and warps your view of its benefits.

We are at an advantage over our dog companions because we can speak. We can reason with ourselves and with each other. We have the ability to explain reasons that we feel help is needed. We discuss pros and cons. Another fantastic advantage that humans have over dogs is the ability to seek individual help. A sick dog can't borrow your keys and drive itself to the vet when it feels a bit nauseated, but should your mate absolutely refuse to seek help with you when things begin to fall apart, as humans we are capable of getting help for and by ourselves. Though not ideal to try to fix yourself and another person without that other person being present, any help getting insight into yourself and how you function in a relationship is better than no insight at all. In the end, you only have control over yourself. You only have control over your actions, your responses, and your decisions.

A change in ourselves can affect all those around us. A random stranger paying for your latte in the Starbucks line can lead to hours of patrons paying it forward. A kind word to your mate when you recognize they are baiting you into an argument might not make any difference the first time. It might not even make a difference the first five times, but you are taking this as an opportunity to grow yourself and hopefully grow the marriage. You working to become more productive in your half of the marriage could inspire him to do the same. You are realizing that you are worthy of better than the situation you are in now and hope that by going to therapy you can better this circumstance and elevate it to what you both deserve.

If this personal growth doesn't help to facilitate a better marital environment then know that it is not for nothing. Even if you become one of the statistics that seeks counseling and gets divorced, everything you learn about yourself will help you in the future. It will help you pick a more compatible mate. It will empower you to not make the same mistakes as you move forward. It will help you and this more suitable future mate resolve the same issues that are destroying you and your current mismatch. It will help and everyone needs help.

Seek help. Seek help early. Try to seek help together, but seek help alone if necessary. Admit your pet is sick and take it to the doctor.

When Is It Time To Euthanize?

I hate when people say they are going to put a pet "to sleep". I know exactly what you mean. While it is meant to be soothing to those who have to make a dreadful decision, I have seen children deeply confused and frightened by this saying as well as adults. In the clinic we use the term euthanize. This may sound like harsh medical terminology, but the word is derived from Greek meaning "Good Death". It envelops both of the truths about this sequence of events. We want it to be good, to be calm, and to be tranquil, but we also need to acknowledge that this is in fact a death. It is an occasion where a living being you love will pass from this life to whatever you think is next. This happens when you make a decision to care for your companion at the expense of a piece of your heart. It is a decision that they will not return from, and it is a casualty you will never forget. I think it a shame to trivialize this experience by comparing it to the slumber we complete every day.

When a client comes into the clinic to euthanize a beloved pet, it is a terrible moment in their lives. It is a visit of differing emotions for doctors and technicians. I feel diverged in my approach. I dread this appointment, because of the immense sadness and loss. Many of us are mourning along with you. We were there for the first visit and have held them close during vaccines, telling you and them it was going to be ok. We have nervously watched over their heartbeat during surgeries. We have nursed and coddled them when they were sick. No, we are not their parents. We understand there is a difference in the hurt you are feeling and our own sorrow. We are not their owners, but we are their friends, and we are also saying goodbye.

Contrary to that, I also adore the chance to support another person in this endeavor. It is at this moment that you see the true heart of a puppy-parent and get to ensure that this visit, the last visit, is peaceful. I get to hear stories as we are preparing about how they picked this pet out of a litter after seeing it was the only one in a colored ribbon, because it had stolen the other ribbons off all the other puppies. I heard about the funny moments when this dog knocked over the Christmas tree and the time it ate an entire loaf of bread. I have listened to heartwarming tales of when the owner was going through chemo, and the dog slept just outside the door for weeks since it was not allowed in the room. I have watched a recently married woman weep and smiles while she affectionately describes this pet as her "first husband."

Most importantly, I am given the opportunity to assure the client that they are doing the right thing. There is nothing worse that the fear and stress that an undecided heart brings. I can hold a person's hand and look them in the eye, confidently stating from a medical perspective, "You are doing the right thing". This doesn't make it easier or any less upsetting. It doesn't take away the pain of losing a dear friend whom you loved, or the guilt that you sometimes couldn't stand to be around them. It doesn't take away the emptiness. It doesn't make it any less scary to know that when they leave and head home, they will be alone. But what it does do is give them the peace of mind to know that someone else looked at their circumstances and agreed with the decision they are making.

You need this kind of peace when ending a relationship as well. It helps to have a friend agree with you, but in the end you will need to truly believe in yourself and regard your reasons as valid without the endorsement of others. You may not know medicine like a veterinarian, so you need to rely on their wisdom. But no one knows you like *you*. As much as you'd love to solely lean on another's opinion, it comes down to the person in the mirror.

There are many reasons we find ourselves facing this final decision, but in a veterinary clinic, when euthanasia is considered, we look at three things:

pain, health, and quality of life. These are always our deciding factors. Consider these same things with yourself.

Is this relationship painful? Do I feel like I am always the one getting hurt or taken advantage of? Do I feel like I start or lose every argument? Do we both work to fix our problems or are we avoiding them until the next fight where I will end up on the crying end again?

Is this relationship healthy? Is there physical, emotional, or verbal abuse? Am I being cheated on? Do I have a real connection with this person, and am I happy, truly happy, with no "buts" for the majority of our time together? Am I going through the motions to not be alone despite the fact that I know this is not working?

Do I have sufficient quality of life? Do I enjoy life with this person? Do I really live when we are together? Despite problems that arise, am I better because of them? Do I see myself with them when we are old? Do I see myself taking care of him when he can't? Would he do the same for me?

When euthanizing a pet, it is easy to understand that you are the caretaker, and it is your responsibility to make the decision your pet cannot. When deciding to end a relationship we forget that we are our own caretakers, and it is our own responsibility to make decisions that no one else can make for us. Just like you are your pets' best advocate for health and happiness, you must learn how to be that for yourself. You would think nothing of going to bat for your whiskered comrade. Be bold! Harness the power of the Beastie Boys, and fight for your right. It could be the right to party, but primarily the right to be happy again. You deserve this. You are worthy of bliss.

On your way to finding this joy, seek your peace along the way. In the search for this peace you will lament. You will mourn over conversations that never existed and the future you will not have. You will feel abandoned, despite the fact that this was your choice, and you will feel angry at the loneliness that you chose. These perceptions are precisely why you must be at peace with your decision. No one else will have to endure this bombardment of inner monologues and misplaced emotion, and while everyone else can tell you that you will get through it, no one else can believe it for you.

All of those people you turn to during this time- your friends, your colleagues, your family- will be going through this process alongside you. Let me spend some time talking to you, the friends of a person who is considering relationship euthanasia. You will be a haven of safe expression and a shoulder to cry on. You will also find yourself treated like the bane of their existence and a punching bag just bracing for the next hit. You will find yourselves surrounded by a few probable circumstances when it comes to you and your closest friends. Few of them end up with you on the winning end for long.

Option one will end with you and your friend's relationship closer than ever before. She will ask your opinion, and you will give it. She will then take your sententious advice and you will hug. You will come out of the other end of this breakup tunnel skipping into the sunshine. I cannot express just how unlikely this is to happen.

More likely is Option Two where your friend, let's call them SadFace Von Wishy-washy, will beg you for advice and then want to argue every point about how your opinion is wrong. This is a fun one. It's the one where you are a horrible friend. You don't believe in their spouse. They slam you with a series of questions, and they present you with scenarios. They then want you to critique each of these scenarios and tell them what you would do. You try to be careful and give conservative advice. This advice that you give will of course be ignored, but, nonetheless, it must be repeated multiple times. And as you will find out, you are wrong and you end up alone because they think you are giving useless advice on purpose.

In a surprising twist, in Option Three, you end up alone. This time because you did not worry about the conservative advice and you gave the honest answer that was explicitly asked for. You know this one. It's where SadFace avoids you for a minimum of four days because five days ago she asked you for advice during one or more interrogations on her floundering marriage (insert dating). She told you she *truly* wanted to know what you thought about the fact that her new husband hid thousands of dollars of debt from her or that he has been corresponding with his ex girlfriend, and then you told her *exactly* what you thought. That was your first and last mistake in this conversation, because when you do tell her that this is shit, *you* are the one that is cut off. Welcome to being a friend.

Does this mean you should lie? Should you placate her and defend him? Does it mean you should say all the things that you are thinking behind her back? Those questions are difficult to answer. I've never been one to hide my true feelings, at the expense of quite a few nights spent in the midst of Option Three. One of my most valuable lessons on answering these questions, I learned from being hit on by frat guys at a fantastic little bar that used to host two-dollar pint nights every Tuesday. As our version of Cheers, it was where my roommate and I frequented weekly for a solid nine months at the age of twenty-one. We would raid each other's closets for low-cut shirts to ensure free drinks and race to the bar immediately after downing two shots each in the kitchen of our duplex, because "the alcohol wouldn't be in our system yet so it is safe to drive". The logic of the young should make you be ecstatic to be an adult.

These immature frat boys taught me what I now know to be a practice so common it has been mentioned in movies and television shows. Men will compliment and then insult. Some endearing examples of this baboon-like behavior are "I really like that you aren't like the hot psychos I normally go for" or "you have such a pretty face", or a favorite of mine, "not a lot of girls look so good with curves".

When modifying this "compliment and insult" technique to discussing your friend's upcoming euthanasia, I break it down into three pieces. Take care to replace the insult part of this formula with your honest opinion and be sure to include her Neanderthal of a mate in the compliment. I also like to throw in a term of endearment and finish with a piece of fact. An example of starting this would be, "If you really want to know what I think, then he is a complete loser who will always put drinking with his friends before you, and I am quite certain he's fucking that girl that he works with who is just a friend." Part one completed. You got it off your chest. Don't you feel better? I can feel the relief radiating from you now that you have expressed your true feelings at how your friend is being treated. This may seem petty, but in order for you to continue to listen to tear-and-wine-soaked stories of how Cro-Magnon man didn't invite her to the Delta Delta Delta reunion kegger, you need to vent those feelings of protective hatred.

Part two can prove more challenging. Attempting to rationally compliment the man who continually leaves your friend in tears can ignite the fiery pits of sisterly rage within you. A foolproof method is to repeat back all of the asinine compliments your friend uses to defend her man. Saying things she has already stated will reinforce that you do in fact care and listen, which you do. Blanket statements about love and hope work well to get your point across while still making it sound like you truly are rooting for them to make it. Lastly, I tend to throw in the term of endearment because, sweetheart, I'm from Texas. The second part continues as follows: "Honey, I know you love him, and I believe that he loves you too. I have seen you be great together. Like when he drove a hundred miles to fix your flat tire, or bought all of us manicures so you wouldn't have to go to the salon alone." Now that wasn't as degrading as you thought it would be. It was all true. You *have* seen them be great together. You do know that they both love each other. You did get a great shellac manicure for free. But you can love someone and still be wrong for him or her.

Let's move to part three with rounded out facts. "But you are miserable and crying constantly, and this relationship is not working for you or him. If he isn't brave enough to make a change for the better then you have to be." This statement is what it all boils down to. These words are what you really wanted to say all along, and now you have. Now you stop! Trust me. Just stop. Now is not the time to berate her and repeat this twenty-seven times. She knows. She knew before you said it, and to continue to drill regret into her is what puts you into Option Three as the Mayor of Aloneville. In addition, it's also just cruel. The self - restraint to stop is what took me the longest to learn.

After you have spoken your truths, you shut up and listen to hers. You pour her wine and let her cry.

You support the decision that she may or may not make, and you understand that it is hers to make. Just like it was yours when you were the one with the mascara-stained eyes.

Whether or not there is the decision to euthanize, you as the friend or you as the owner of this relationship have many rough days ahead. It does get better, and the hurt lessens every day, but you already know that. It doesn't make it any easier. It does, however, give us an excuse to fill that water bowl up with wine.

The Tail End: A Conclusion

When you write a book, you always wonder what people will think. When you write a book like this, one based on stories experienced by yourself or the people closest to you, you don't wonder so much what random people will think. You do wonder if you will have any actual friends who will answer your phone calls once they read the book. I did one thing as I was writing this memoir that I hoped would help ease a few friends' minds. Next to the title of each chapter, in the margins of the first printed draft of this book, I made a point to scribble the names of each of the lovely and strong women who experienced the atrocities that inspired that chapter. At the top of virtually each miniature list was my own name. The truth of this book is exactly as I stated in the introduction. If there was a dilemma that only one of my sisters-in-arms experienced, then I left it on the cutting room floor.

The most surprising part of hearing the responses to this book were that every one of my close friends fell into one of two categories: the ones who saw themselves in every single chapter and wanted to be horribly offended by my misuse of their pasts or the ones who saw all of their friends on the pages, but didn't see themselves at all because they apparently live in a fantasy world. In this Narnia, they are perfect and would never conceive of having such horrible experiences.

One friend I imagine will call me crying when she finally reads this. She will be ashamed and embarrassed that I had betrayed her trust by sharing her stories for the world to see. She will not want to hear my explanations or my accounts. She won't want to see the other names on my list next to chapter titles that she knows are about solely her, and she won't want to see that her name was missing from the chapters she was most offended by.

One friend read a rough draft and called me to sing my praises. She told me how proud she was to be my friend. She said she was inspired by what I had accomplished. After her initial acclaim of my work, her only other response before pausing for my reply was "Wow! *So and So* really takes a beating in this book!" This friend on the phone, in particular, was actually the subject of quite a few more chapters than *So and So*.

I truly aspired to write a book that would help my friends understand they are not alone, and help myself realize that as well. I wanted them to know that we have all made immature choices. We all stayed with guys that we knew were terrible for us until those men left and threw us into a shame spiral. We have all walked a hypocritical line where we knew how much smarter we were than our friends. We watched as they devalued themselves for a man that was beneath them and as they stayed because they were "in love". I wanted them to know that we all reach a place of intelligence where, despite how much we wanted to be with a man we truly loved, we left him because we knew he was less than we deserved. We owe our friends thanks for instilling in us the confidence we needed to leave him, even if we would never let you know how much it hurt us to do so. We all strive so hard to make our friends proud that sometimes we push them away.

I wrote this book after years of repeating to my friends, co-workers, and husband that men and dogs were more alike than anyone knew. I'd rattle off my experiences and advice to those who asked for it, or didn't, and follow it with "I'm going to write a book, I swear". Then, one day I woke up and just started typing. I'm really proud of myself. These pages aren't filled with words you have to Google to know the definition. Some of these chapters are probably things you have heard at least once or seven times, even if it didn't include the dog metaphors, but that probably means you need to hear it again. I know this book is not going to win a Pulitzer, but in writing this book, I've dissected down to the root of many of my insecurities. I feel like I've become a better wife and a better friend. I have learned a considerate amount about my relationships with men and a lot more about myself.

The male figures in my life that I have trusted most and have been inspired by more than any other have been canine in nature. Cats could take you or leave you most of the time, but I am proud to admit that I thrive on the constant reassurance that my dog provides. I want and need to feel loved even when I know I am not at my best, and my dog will give me that. My longest relationship with a male is my eleven-year-old rat terrier, Argyle. I have known this pup since he was six weeks old when he belonged to a friend of mine from college. He officially became mine at about seven months old. He is currently acting as an armrest as I type. I am in debt with this dog. If I leave the room, he will follow. He has been with me through every life goal. Relationships, career changes, purchasing a house, marriage. He is devoted to me. My husband often laments that if I were nowhere to be found, Args would wither away. Incidentally, Argyle is not really mentioned in this book's anecdotes, because he is perfect. And he in no way sets an unobtainable standard for future dogs. Just kidding, he totally does.

Argyle has some serious health issues. He has small disc spaces in his neck and thoracic spine. In addition, he has an active form of epilepsy, which makes it impossible to perform surgery on the small disc spaces. Even with my extensive knowledge of veterinary medicine and the life expectancies of canines with my dog's illnesses, it is hard for me to think of a time when I won't have him following me from room to room, only to return to the couch where we started a few minutes later. God forbid I be out of his sight for more than thirty seconds. He would never voluntarily leave my side if I didn't physically prevent him from doing so. I have thought long and hard about what my decisions for him hold. I know that he will progress in his prognosis of disc and neurologic illness into a state that provides us with good days and bad days. Eventually those bad days will overtake the good days and will require that I make a decision. I dread this with my whole being.

I realized while dissecting my relationships with humans, and my relationships with dogs, that what I am experiencing with my first husband, Argyle, is exactly what I am always faced with when I deal with all men. I will have good days and I will have bad days in any relationship. I will have days that make me understand why I have made the choice to keep us together, and I will have days where I feel terrible about dragging out this inevitable ending. I know now that every day that I choose to be with a man is exactly that, a choice.

I appreciate now because of my dog that I deserve more happy days than sad ones. Just as my dog is, I deserve someone who is happy to see me when I get home from work. I realize that I deserve someone who wants to make my life as comfortable as possible. I understand that I am so lucky to have one person that makes my world whole. When he leaves, I am less than I should be. I want to be with that person in every room of my life so that we can protect each other. I know that I will follow him to the ends of the Earth, if only to follow him back to where we started.

When you are comfortable with yourself and confident in a healthy relationship, you will recognize all of these same things about the special person that you have found, like I did, and that person will feel the same way as you do.

... Or you'll realize you're a cat person.